WE EXIST

By

Tanita Allen

Disclaimer

All contents copyright © 2023

Table of Contents

Dedication

This book is dedicated to all the HD Warriors: The ones in the past who shaped me, the one in the present who nurture me, and the ones in the future who await me.

These are the individuals who inspire me to fight every day and made writing this book worthwhile.

Foreword

Within these pages are the most defining events of my life. These events have changed every aspect of my being, from my hopes and aspirations to the way I perceive the world. Starting from 2006, when I left my home in Cleveland to move to New York, this book follows the series of unpredictable occurrences triggered by this decision, leading to the most unexpected of all – a diagnosis of Huntington's disease.

According to prevailing medical knowledge at the time, a black person does not get Huntington's, nor should the symptoms be as pronounced as mine were at such an early age. Yet there I was a black woman with early onset Huntington's now face these false preconceptions. My very existence set the stage for a tortuous struggle where my race amplified every challenge I faced, from accessing the treatment I so desperately needed to the legalities of holding the parties responsible for the early onset. My tale unveils all these systemic inequities ingrained in our healthcare and legal systems, shedding light on the burdens carried by those standing in the margins.

This book bears witness to those lowest moments of my life, the despair and depression, the uphill climb through medical entanglements, the legal battle, and the uncountable hurdles that obstructed my path to healing and justice. Yet, in the face of these challenges, there is another thread because my story is not just about my illness.

These pages also chronicle my strength and resilience in the face of so many adversaries who tried to diminish my existence. As you read about the darkness I face, you will also see how I found the fortitude to face my mortality, made peace with an uncertain future, and emerged with a newfound appreciation for the beauty of life.

Make no mistake, this book is not about victimhood, nor is it just a memoir recounting personal difficulties. It is a lantern lighting the way for others facing their own shadows. It is an invitation to find strength in the face of adversity, to forge ahead with determination, and to believe unwaveringly in the potential for a brighter tomorrow. It is a declaration of empowerment – a journey about reclaiming agency over your life, standing tall and declaring to the world, "WE EXIST!"

As you accompany me through these chapters of my life, I hope you draw inspiration from my experiences to find the strength to endure, overcome, and ultimately thrive in your own life.

Chapter 1: It Starts Like Any Other Story

It is strange where your life can start and where you end up. My childhood would not have given you a single clue about the struggles I would face as an adult. When I think back, my early days almost seem idyllic. I was the middle child in a regular middle-class family. Growing up in Cleveland, it was my parents with me and my brother and sister. My siblings and I played, laughed, and fought, just like all siblings around the world.

There was none of that middle-child neglect or any emotional trauma. I went to catholic school until freshman year. Even catholic school was uneventful. Yes, the teachers were strict, and there were all rules to follow, but it was all bearable. When I started my sophomore year in a public school, you would think something to write about must have happened. But even my last few years in high school were normal and problem-free.

On top of this, I had no major health problems, serious injuries, or hospital visits. I didn't even have any unusual, incurable symptoms or knowledge of any family medical history that needed special attention. Now, I know people say that when you look back into the past, it is with rose-tinted glasses, and everything seems perfect and blissful. But trust me when I say I am not blinded by nostalgia. Things were good back then, and I thank God for a safe and healthy start in life.

When I finished high school, I decided to work in sales. Working in sales is one of those jobs where you spend your day interacting with people. I enjoyed this. I liked interacting with others, listening to their needs, and helping them wherever possible.

Yes, a career in sales sounded promising to me, and that's where I thought I would stay. But let me remind you, we are not the masters of our destiny. Oh no, my friend. Everything you think you know can go right out the window, and you can find yourself in uncharted territory. My story was about to take a dramatic turn, and I was utterly unprepared.

It was 2006, and I was in a long-distance relationship with a man I had met on a previous trip to NYC. Let's call him Andrew. I met him most randomly. I was asking for directions, but we got to talking. The next thing you know, we are exchanging numbers. I was heading back home soon, so to be honest, I really didn't think this chance meeting had the potential to become some grand love story. And yet we stayed in touch, talking over the phone whenever we could. Let me remind you that this was a time before everyone and their grandma had a cell phone. We are talking about landlines, answering machines, and long-distance phone bills. There were no video calls, no location tracking, and all that.

You just had to trust the person on the other end was being honest with you, and based on that, you built a relationship. Trust me, making a long-distance relationship work during that time took real effort. You really had to make time for the other person. You know what I did? I packed up my stuff, said goodbye to family and friends, and moved all the way to New York! And yes, I did it for the guy. I thought we were ready to take our relationship to the next level, live together, and create a life.

And really, it just made sense for me to be the one to move. New York offered a lot more in terms of education and jobs than my hometown. That's not to say that Cleveland has no opportunities. There is a lot someone can do in Ohio. But I think at that time I wanted a change too.

So here I was, moving into my boyfriend's apartment in Washington Heights, and it was something, to say the least. Now, I'm not saying that I was expecting a penthouse suite. I have never been one to demand luxury, but there are some basic comforts every person desires. Case in point: Andrew's apartment was on the fourth floor of a building with no elevator. I will never forget those flights of stairs. There were days that I dreaded having to leave the apartment because it meant I would have to climb all those steps when I got back. But that's how it was with these old apartment buildings. They didn't have the facilities we now consider necessary.

The area that Andrew lived in was known as the Little Dominican Republic, and you really felt like you were in a different country because hardly anyone spoke English. On top of that, there was crime and there were drugs. I am sure any other woman in my situation would have looked at all this and taken it as a sign to grab the first flight out of there. But like I said, I was a woman in love, completely blinded by it, so I chose to make a new life for myself here.

As I've mentioned before, I enjoy interacting and helping others, so this new city was the perfect place for me to find a more fulfilling career path. That's how I decided to go to New York Paralegal School and become a paralegal. I graduated a year later, in 2007, and right away, I was hired by a New York federal court. At this court, I worked in the administrative department with attorneys, and I really enjoyed myself there. I loved the work I was doing. It was stimulating and worthwhile. I truly felt like I was a part of something bigger and helping people with their lives. Not only was the work fascinating, but the work environment and the people around me were also outstanding.

It wasn't one of those cutthroat offices where people pulled each other down. There was a real sense of camaraderie, like being part of a family. I made many friends there, and my time working there was the highlight of my day.

Just when things were at their best, and I was comfortable and happy, fate threw me a curveball. Then life started to go downhill. The first thing that was hit was my work when I was moved to a second courthouse in 2008. I can honestly say it was like leaving heaven and going to hell. I am not even exaggerating. The people in my new workplace were toxic, hostile, and petty. They were so bad I won't even call them my colleagues. There was no collaboration or encouragement. It was just a competition all the time.

To make matters worse, my supervisor was just plain mean, like the devil incarnate. She didn't like me, and she didn't hide it. I was a trained paralegal, and she had me doing actual labor - can you imagine? That is not what a paralegal does. And don't think for a minute it was because there was no one else who could do it. There were plenty of stronger, more capable people right there who could have done the heavy lifting, but no, she always targeted me and made me do it. To this day, I don't know what her issue was with me. There is nothing sadder than women who pull other women down.

To add insult to injury, my relationship with Andrew had reached its limit. Turns out he was a womanizing jerk with multiple girlfriends around town. Heartbroken doesn't even begin to cover how I felt when I found out. It was like someone had stabbed me directly in the heart. When I look back at that time, all I can think about is how naïve I was.

Then again, everyone says hindsight is 20/20, and we see red flags much clearer after a relationship implodes. It sucks, but there is nothing more you can do except move on. And that is exactly what I did. I wasn't going to waste any more of my time on that fool. He had stolen two and a half years of my life, and I was done. I moved on, and I moved out to my own place in 2009.

The apartment I found was on Craigslist, and I know what you are thinking right now - who uses Craigslist? Yes, that site is shady now. But let me tell you that back in 2009, it was reliable, and you could really find some good deals. Of course, at that time, I was desperate. I wanted to get out of Andrew's apartment as soon as possible, so any half-decent apartment was a deal to me. I wasn't checking things like if the building was up to code and stuff like that. It was just about the rent.

The one I finally took was in a hundred-year-old building, and just like all the other old buildings in Washington Heights, it didn't have an elevator, just my luck. But this time, I was on the second floor, so it was definitely much more manageable, but the rent was higher than I would have liked. It was $1650 a month – a lot for an apartment in 2009. But it was better than Andrew's place and twice as big. Although it was more space than I needed, I thought I could get a roommate in the future to help cover the rent.

There was one thing off about the apartment, though a strange, persistent smell inside. It's hard to describe precisely what it was except to say it was pungent. The problem was that I had no reference to compare that smell to, so when I was told it was the smell of new paint, I believed it. Remember, I was desperate to move out. The building could have been half on fire, and I still would have considered moving in. When the super said the smell would eventually fade away, I went with it and didn't give it another thought.

Do you remember how I said at the beginning that I had been a healthy child and never had any medical problems my entire life? Well, that was still held true when I first moved to New York and lived in Andrew's apartment. I mean, there was the occasional flu and the seasonal cold here and there, but nothing to go to the ER. Well, that healthy streak was over when I moved into my new place.

It was like 30 years of illness had hit me. I was sick all the time, and there were so many unexplainable symptoms. I was having breathing problems. My nose was bleeding, and I was losing my hair like I was going through chemo. I was dizzy all the time, and the constant non-stop nausea was killing me. I felt like I could throw up any time, all the time. I knew I was dealing with a lot of stress in my life, what with my job, breaking up, and moving, but I was certain these symptoms I had were not stress-related. Something was very wrong, and I was scared.

In 2009, no one was Googling their symptoms or researching illnesses. We just went to the doctor and accepted what they said. The problem was, every time I went to the ER, they told me I was fine and sent me on my way without doing any blood tests, x-rays, or actual examinations. My life had transformed into a never-ending cycle of walking in and out of the ER like I was stuck in a revolving door. To make matters worse, doctors didn't even try to piece the symptoms together to figure out what was going on with my body. They just labeled me a drug addict and an alcoholic. I cannot even begin to describe the frustration I felt. It was like physical pain. To these medical professionals, I was invisible, and I know that the color of my skin played a big role in that. That's just the way our healthcare is built. There is a racial bias that stops them from taking Black people seriously. It's deeply engraved in them since the days of doing medical experiments on black slaves.

But these medical issues were just one aspect of my life. Along with all this, I was still going to work. I have bills to pay and couldn't afford to quit. Every morning, I forced myself out of bed and went down to the courthouse. There was no denying I was sick, and I couldn't hide it. I looked ill, but my sadistic supervisor didn't give a damn. She could see, plain as day, that I wasn't well, but still, she targeted me and had me doing all the labor work.

My career suddenly ended one day when she made me lift a very heavy box. As I picked it up, I heard something pop in my back. It was a terrifying sound, and I had to go to the ER. The doctors told me that I had a bulging disc in my spine and I would need long-term physical therapy with a sports medicine doctor and take medication for the pain.

But even this incident wasn't rock bottom. While in the ER, I was questioned about what had happened, so I told them what happened and how I got hurt at work. Little did I know that the ER would flag my injury as a workplace injury, and I was now required to report it for insurance purposes. I followed the proper protocol, I am a paralegal, after all, and I filed a worker's compensation claim. Imagine my surprise when I was called down to the HR department of the federal court and told that if I went through with this claim, I would be fired. It was the most ridiculous thing I have ever heard, and I was dumbfounded. I even told HR at the time that what they were doing was illegal. They agreed but said they could do whatever they wanted. The audacity was shocking.

Regardless of their callous attitude, I knew I was in the right, so I went through and reported my worker's compensation. Sure enough, a month later, I was called in and fired by the same person who told me he would fire me the first time.

I wasn't going to stand for this kind of treatment, and I appealed in court. I made a big decision and decided to represent myself. I knew it was risky, but I had all the facts, and no one could deny the evidence. So, I presented my case to the judge professionally and thoroughly. The federal court had no right to fire me, and I wouldn't let them get away with this. And guess what? I won! The court ruled in my favor and declared that I should be given my old job back as well as one year of pay and have all my medical and dental benefits reinstated.

This verdict was like a ray of sunlight, and I was elated, but the employers at the federal court found a loophole. They let me come back alright but not to my old job. I was now classified as a retired government person, so I got a pension and medical benefits. While this arrangement actually turned out for the best because of my medical issues, I didn't like it one bit. I wanted to work and build a career, but I couldn't because I was so sick. My life felt like it was over. I was depressed, miserable, and crying all the time.

This was when the neurological symptoms reared their ugly head. I started having these unexplainable, random muscle spasms. One time, it happened in front of my sports doctor, Dr. V, during one of my regular physical therapy sessions for my back injury. Dr. V noticed my toes were moving. He asked if I was making them move. I told him I wasn't and thought they were just muscle spasms. I'll never forget his response to this. Dr. V looked me straight in the eye and said that this was not a muscle issue. He said something was wrong with my brain and I needed to see a neurologist immediately.

I didn't think things could get any worse. Turns out I had never been more wrong in my life.

Chapter 2: The Beginning of the End

The year 2010 started with me at home without a job. I spend my time online, searching for neurologists in New York. After my session with Dr. V, I called every name I could find to locate a doctor who would see me as quickly as possible. Many of them were booked months in advance, and it took some time, but finally, I managed to get an appointment with Dr. F, a neurologist at Mount Sinai Hospital, a well-known New York medical facility.

I like the atmosphere at Mount Sinai. It was nice and clean but still open and bright. I remember many people were in the lobby, but it wasn't overwhelming, so I wasn't scared or anxious to be there. The staff was pleasant and helpful, and I went in optimistic, thinking I would find answers. I met with Dr. F and a female resident. I was used to other doctors in the exam room, so I didn't mind her being there. Luckily for me, Dr. F was well-mannered and friendly. He listened closely to everything I told him about my medical history and symptoms, then showed him how my toes were moving on their own.

Dr. F did a neurological exam to check my nervous system and brain activity. This involved taking a blunt instrument and running it up and down my legs and foot. He repeated this on different parts of my lower body and kept asking if I could feel it. Then, he asked me to perform a variety of movements to check my command over my body. I remember walking in a straight line with one foot in front of the other, opening and closing my eyes, and following his finger. Everything seemed to be in order because I was able to do everything he asked.

Finally, when he started examining my toes, I could see him getting excited with their movement, even asking if he could make a video and record it, which I let him do. After this neurological exam, Dr. F told me that he suspected I had a condition known as painful leg and moving toe (PLMT) syndrome. I had never heard of it, as I am sure is the case with many others.

PLMT was such an extremely rare disorder that I had to look it up online after I got home. According to my research, people who suffer from PLMT syndrome have jerky leg or toe movements that they cannot control, and it is usually accompanied by pain. Now, I had no pain in my legs or toes at the time. The PLMT only seemed to explain the wiggling toes, but none of my other symptoms. Still, Dr. F was convinced by his diagnosis. However, before he prescribed any medication, he wanted me to see another doctor at Columbia Presbyterian who could confirm his findings. This doctor, Dr. G, was Dr. F's mentor and a very well-respected neurologist in New York.

So, a couple of weeks later, I found myself in the neurological department at Columbia Presbyterian, which turned out to be a completely different experience from Mount Sinai. This ward was isolated from the main hospital and felt like an institution, cold and uninviting. There were people there, but many moved erratically, some with tremors and others in wheelchairs. It was a scary place, and it made me even more anxious about my situation. As uncomfortable as the hospital was, Dr. G was even worse. He was rude and dismissive. I didn't like him from the moment I walked into his examination room.

"Boy, you are overweight. You need to lose weight." That was the first thing he said when he saw me. All I could do was stare back at him in shock.

Was this man, who was supposed to be one of the best neurologists in the city, body-shaming me? Looking back, I should have said something and stood up for myself, but what he said was so unexpected that I didn't know how to respond. I ignored his comment, told him about my symptoms, and showed him how my toes moved. Like Dr. F before him, Dr. G did a similar exam, running a blunt tool up and down my leg to check for my nerve response and having me perform a series of movements. In the end, he also agreed with the PLMT syndrome diagnosis. Still, he did not prescribe any medication either.

Here, I have to mention that both these doctors made their diagnoses after doing a neurological exam. That's it. There were no blood tests, no CT scans, or MRIs done. Whenever I retell these experiences to others, they always ask me why these doctors didn't do any other tests. Honestly, I don't know why. They were so sure of their diagnosis, and I believed them because that's what patients should do. We are supposed to trust the doctor in the white coat. So, I didn't push for any other tests either.

At first, I thought these two doctors had figured out my medical problem, but then my fingers started moving on their own. Then, the upper part of my body began to twist to the side. I knew that this was not PLMT syndrome. Something else was going on. I went back to Dr. G and showed him these new symptoms. But he was convinced I was moving my body myself, and no matter what I told him, he would not let go of the PLMT syndrome diagnosis. This highly respected doctor actually believed that from the waist down, I had painful leg and moving toe syndrome, and from the waist up, I had a psychological problem. Apparently, there was nothing else he, as a neurologist, could do for me, so I should see a psychiatrist.

Now, when I think back to this moment, I can't help but laugh because the whole thing was so absurd. I am not a doctor, I didn't go to medical school, but even I know you can't just pick a disease or disorder and force it on a patient. You have to examine them in every way possible until you can find an explanation for most of their symptoms, not just one. I had a boatload of issues, but so far, the two doctors I had visited were only concerned with one of them: my moving toes. Even though I knew in my gut I didn't have any mental illness, I still went to see a psychiatrist. I was scared. I was desperate. My body was moving on its own, and I needed to know what was going on. I won't lie. A tiny part of me thought maybe Dr. G was right, so I scheduled an appointment with a New York psychiatrist, Dr. C.

I should have never fallen for Dr. G's ridiculous diagnosis. Sure enough, it only took Dr. C three sessions to figure out that there was nothing psychologically wrong with me. I was so relieved to hear this because it meant I wasn't going crazy. Yes, my body was still moving involuntarily, but at least I knew for certain now that it wasn't all in my head. I needed to find a new neurologist because there was no way I was going back to Dr. G. That man was a quack, in my opinion. I needed someone who would take me and my symptoms seriously.

And so began my quest to find a good doctor. I must have seen at least ten different ones, some in hospitals, others at their private practice. But it was so hopeless. Most of them would see I had been to Dr. G and half agreed with his half PLMT syndrome, half psychological diagnosis. It was like Dr. G had some bizarre hold over all the neurologists in New York. No one wanted to disagree with his diagnosis. They kept saying *if Columbia Presbyterian says you have it, you must have it.*

Along with these yes-men doctors, there were also some who were just plain incompetent. I clearly remember seeing a certain Russian doctor who, during a neurological exam, told me to leave because *it was time for me to go* after I fell to the ground while trying to walk in a straight line. He was the least bit concerned with why I fell. He just wanted me gone. I left each doctor with tears in my eyes, disheartened, exhausted, and frustrated.

While all this was going on, I was still in and out of the ER because I didn't know what else to do about my body's movements. By this time, I had also developed facial and vocal tics too. My face started flinching by itself, and I was making these weird, guttural noises that I could not control.

Every time I went to the ER, all the healthcare providers would say was to *follow up with a neurologist, follow up with a neurologist* like a broken record. They gave me medication to stop my body from moving. I didn't know at the time, but it was just Ativan, also known as *lorazepam*, a drug used to help people with anxiety disorder, insomnia, seizures, nausea, and vomiting. It was a temporary fix for me, reducing the frequency of momvents, but also made me drowsy and confused. I couldn't focus on nor remember very well what was happening around me when I was on it. All I knew was I needed to get home quickly. Otherwise, I would be too out of it to do much else.

My body would stay still during the night, and I would go to sleep, but in the morning, I would wake up, and the involuntary movements would start again, and I would have to go back to the ER. It was never-ending. I hated going to the ER at Columbia Presbyterian, but I had no choice because it was the closest one to my place.

That place felt like a warzone. There were gunshot patients and stabbing victims around me, the staff was rude, and the nurses were mean. They took one look at me, saw a black woman, and immediately assumed I was another crackhead from the streets looking for another high. They would test me for alcohol, crack, cocaine, and all of that. Of course, all these tests would come up negative because I wasn't a drug addict, but it didn't matter. The healthcare workers there were too biased and racist to listen to me.

It's hard writing about this time because I was overwhelmed with depression. My medical issues had taken over my life. My body was failing me, I thought I was dying, and the doctors couldn't help me. I had no close friends or family around me either in NYC. There was always this dark cloud over my head, and I was miserable.

When I would talk to my mom and tell her I wanted to come home, she would always say to stay in New York because that is where I would find answers. But it seemed like there were no answers here, just ignorant doctors who were not listening to me and not taking my condition seriously. It didn't help that I still didn't have a job, so there was nothing to distract me.

But then the ultimate distraction came. Just when I thought it couldn't get any worse, I discovered an invisible evil slowly poisoning me.

Chapter 3: The Silent Killer

Let's take a moment to go back to my apartment. Remember, I moved into this apartment in August 2009, and there was a questionable odor from the second I walked into that space. When I asked the landlord about it, he wrote it off as the smell of paint. I assumed he knew what he was talking about, and I didn't give it a second thought. Well, after nearly two years, that smell was still there. Every time I walked in through my front door, it would hit me. I was certain this odor wasn't paint because those fumes eventually faded away. This was something else. Along with the smell, I was having some other problems in my apartment. For one, my gas stove did not work properly.

For those who are unaware, natural gas (methane) is used all over the country in gas stoves and boilers. In New York, gas supply pipes run through the gas meters in all the older buildings, but they carry a lot of serious issues:

1. Natural gas is <u>highly</u> flammable. Even 5% natural gas in the air can cause an explosion. All it needs is a spark or a tiny flame.
2. It is extremely toxic in a closed space because it pushes the oxygen out of the air and causes all kinds of symptoms.
3. When it doesn't burn properly, it produces carbon monoxide, a deadly gas that is colorless and odorless.
4. Even if it is burning properly, natural gas increases carbon emissions in the atmosphere, which is bad for the environment.

Back then, I didn't know all this. I also did not know that according to the NYC housing code, all building gas meters *must* be outside in a well-ventilated area and off the wall. I was living in an apartment with the gas meter inside, in the kitchen, embedded in the wall! I was sleeping in a death trap with so many code violations, and I was completely oblivious. When I had issues with my stove, I didn't realize what it could mean. Never in a million years could I have predicted what would happen.

When my stove problems started, I did what anyone in my situation would do and called my landlord, Mr. S. He sent the superintendent, Mr. J, up to check it out and fix it so it would burn gas. The super got the job done but didn't do it properly. Remember, I lost my job at the beginning of 2010, so I was home much more. This was when all my unexplained symptoms started, and it never occurred to me that my surroundings could be the cause. Even when my carbon monoxide alarm went off in July 2010, it didn't register. It should have, but it didn't because Mr. S said it was a false alarm. I believed my landlord. Why would he lie to me?

Also, I did not have the mental stamina to dig deeper because my health was failing at an alarming rate, and I was on a merry-go-round of doctors. But then the smell got stronger and stronger, and let me tell you, natural gas stinks! Gas companies purposely add a chemical to this odorless gas so it smells and people know it's in the air. In New York City, the gas company adds *mercaptan,* an additive that smells like rotten eggs. With my gas stove and oven constantly malfunctioning and this rotten smell in the air, I hounded Mr. S, who kept sending Mr. J, but it didn't make a difference. The stove still would work, and the unbearable smell wasn't disappearing. There was obviously a gas problem. I knew it, my landlord knew it, but he won't call the gas company.

Instead, he calls a so-called expert who was actually a kitchen appliance repairman. This man suggests the entire stove and oven be replaced but, in the meantime, works on it to see if he can get it running. During all these kitchen and gas issues, my building changed hands, and I have new landlords, Mr. B and Mr. R. By now, I was certain I had a gas leak somewhere, so I called the gas company myself. I had reached my limit with the landlords and their temporary solutions. Looking back, it was a miracle I connected the dots with all my unexplainable medical problems.

Calling the gas company was easy, but getting them to pay attention and send someone immediately was an arduous process. I had to call again and again. Every call was the same: *there is a leak at my place. Send someone to check.* You would think, of all people, the gas company would understand the gravity of the situation, but they took their precious time sending someone over.

Finally, in February 2011, the gas company sent someone to my apartment who immediately knew there was a leak because he could smell the gas. He inspected my apartment with a gas-measuring instrument known as a GMI machine, but his machine did NOT sense the gas and give a reading, which was very strange. Regardless of the faulty device, this technician pressed on and, sure enough, found a leak in the pipe that connected the gas meter to the stove. He shut off the meter valve and locked it, so it wasn't operational. Before leaving, he pulled out a GMI machine to check for any gas in the air – the same faulty one he used before that didn't pick up the gas we could both smell. Why? I don't know. How this man thought a fault machine could give an accurate reading is beyond my understanding, but that was what was happening.

Before leaving, he *red-tagged* my apartment and documented it as an immediate gas hazard. When a gas company red tags your place, they put a physical tag on your meter, meaning a gas leak must be fixed urgently. Another team is supposed to come as soon as possible to remedy the situation. This technician left thinking his job was done.

My new landlord, Mr. R, was furious, but not because of a gas leak. He was angry at me for telling the gas company in the first place because now he was obliged to pay to get it fixed. He was not happy at all. Outraged at the thought of having to spend money, he took me to court. He wanted me evicted. Of course, he couldn't do it because there was no legal precedent. There was a gas leak, and I reported it to the gas company. He is the landlord, so he is responsible for fixing it, plain and simple.

With the gas leak fixed, I thought for the first time in a while, something in my life was solved. But, of course, that was nothing more than wishful thinking. Even after the gas company claimed to have turned the gas off, I could still smell it. My instinct told me there was still a leak, so I was back on the phone. I called the landlord, but he would not listen. He said it was impossible to smell gas because the pipe was shut off. I called the gas company again and again, but they didn't believe me. According to their records, the gas was shut off, so it could not be leaking. To them, I was nothing more than a crazy lady. Nevertheless, I knew what I could smell, so I pushed and kept calling.

Do you know what it is like to know something is 100% true but to be denied that truth by people who are supposed to help you? It is mental torture. You are fighting to be acknowledged when you are invisible. I felt like I was screaming at the top of a mountain, begging to be heard, to be treated with a shred of decency by anyone.

From my health to this gas problem, I was surrounded by thick-skulled people who refused to listen and comprehend what I was telling them. This kind of treatment is inhumane. Everyone deserves to be heard.

Six months later, in July 2011, the city inspector came to inspect my apartment, and guess what? He could smell gas. Thanks to his involvement, the gas company finally paid attention and sent someone that month. Their technician came to my door, and the first thing he said when he came in was *I smell gas!* He used his GMI machine, and it showed a positive reading. There was no doubt anymore. There was gas leaking into my apartment.

He inspected the meter again and was horrified to discover the valve was faulty. Despite the main line being *shut off* since February, it was still letting gas through. This gentleman said I was very lucky because my apartment could have exploded. This time, he made sure to shut it off properly and repeatedly checked to be certain. It wasn't until later that year, in September, that all the gas leaks were fixed. For a total of eight months, I lived with toxic fumes in my house and breathed in that deadly gas. I had no family in the city or friends whose sofa I could crash on. I could not afford to find a new place to live or travel back home. My life at this point felt like I was stuck in quicksand. No matter what I did, I couldn't get free. I just sank deeper and deeper.

The worst part of this whole situation was it was out of my control to fix. I was forced to rely on others, and their incompetence was astounding. Starting with my landlords, let's look at Mr. S, the one in charge when I first moved in. He knew the installation of the gas meter was a code violation. At some point, before I moved in, the kitchen of my apartment was remodeled, and the meter was built into the wall. Maybe those previous owners didn't like the look of it. Who knows.

I can't say if the landlord knew about this renovation at the time, but it is a fact that he eventually found out. Landlords always check apartments after they are vacated, and this building's landlord was not blind. This man could deny knowing about the renovation, but he knew the meter was in the wall when I moved in.

The same goes for the new landlords. Both these parties knew about this first violation. They also knew my carbon dioxide alarm was messed up, another violation. Neither of them got it fixed, another violation. I complained to both of them about my stove not working and the gas smell, but they didn't do anything about it. The violations just keep piling up.

Now we come to the gas company. First of all, they send a meter reader *every month* to record the number of gas units used. These people would walk INTO my apartment and see my gas meter IN THE WALL but never say a word about the illegal installation. They just took down the numbers and walked out. They never commented on the smell that reeked from my apartment – an odor they are TRAINED to recognize.

On top of that, the gas company took their sweet time to address the gas leak, even though they were receiving complaint after complaint and knew full well the dangers of a leak in an apartment building. Then, when they finally come around to it, the gas company sends technicians with broken GMI machines, mind you, who did a half-assed job.

Remember, my meter was red-tagged. That is a BIG deal. If anyone struck even a match in my apartment, it could have ignited the gas and caused a massive fire. And in an apartment building, such a catastrophe could have cost lives. A gas leak complaint is a serious issue that needs to be solved immediately and tripled checked to be sure.

But it was not a serious issue for the gas company, so they did their best: delayed the work and kept their heads in the sand. All I could do was sit there in my deteriorating physical state, breathing in the poison. Their negligence is unforgivable.

Chapter 4: Diagnosis or Death Sentence

While I was battling with my landlords and the gas company, I was getting sicker and sicker. During those months, I started shaking uncontrollably and had to use a walker to move around. I had no appetite and absolutely no clue what was wrong with me.

Between my calls to the gas company, I called Mount Sinai again for another opinion but with a different doctor. I was done with Dr. F, the one who had diagnosed me with the painful leg and moving toe (PLMT) syndrome. I met with Dr. C, another neurologist in their department. She was nice and much more methodical.

She didn't try to force a diagnosis on me, rather working by the process of elimination, meaning instead of figuring out what my medical problem was, she would rule out what it wasn't. This method would narrow the possibilities and help us get closer to an answer.

She ran a battery of tests, from blood tests to MRIs. I was tested for autoimmune diseases, Parkinson's, MS, Sjogren's disease, Lyme disease, Wilson's disease, AIDS, allergies, drugs, and whatnot. The list goes on. For once, I felt like a doctor was trying to help me, and I knew she would find an answer even if it took time.

With the discovery of the gas leaks at home and my symptoms getting worse, I told Dr. C what was happening in my apartment. I knew there was a connection between these two things, even if I didn't understand what it was. That's when Dr. C started asking about my family history and mentioned Huntington's disease.

Huntington's is an inherited disease where the body produces a mutant protein that attacks the brain cells. These attacks lead to permanent nerve damage, which is called *neurodegeneration*. As the condition progresses, symptoms, typically in the later stages of life, start to show.

A person with Huntington's disease eventually loses control of their body and mind. A very accurate genetic test can determine if a person has the genetic marker for Huntington's, and Dr. C suggested I take that test. She told me that it was basically impossible for me to have it as I was African-American. Still, I presented with too many related symptoms for it all to be a coincidence. And since there was no harm in testing, I agreed to it.

And then came the curveball that is always waiting on the sidelines of my life. Turns out, Dr. C worked under Dr. F, and he canceled Huntington's test! Why? According to him, I couldn't have Huntington's because I was black, so the test was a waste of everyone's time.

His racial assumption was based on outdated research done on white people that said only those of European descent could get Huntington's. They had very few cases of the disease in other ethnicities, so they used their limited sample size to make sweeping statements about the condition. Do you want to know why doctors know so little about diseases in the African-American community? It is because of a racial bias and exclusivity in medical research that does not see us as a priority.

The irony of all this is that because of the United States's history of slavery, there is, in fact, a great deal of European ancestry in our blood. Turns out the color of our skin is not enough to determine our ancestry.

At the same time, every disease has its variations and mutations. Every day, the medical field is learning something new, which makes it all the more mind-boggling that a doctor can be so shortsighted. Thankfully, Dr. C did not agree with him, but she couldn't do anything about it because Dr. F was her boss. She insisted I needed to be tested, even if that meant I needed to go to another doctor.

Unfortunately, the bad news wasn't over. There was one more nail to hammer into my coffin. According to Dr. C, whatever was going on with my body was permanent. I would never be able to get rid of it, and it wouldn't get better. *Devastated* doesn't even begin to describe how it felt hearing such words. My doctor had given me a death sentence, and I was utterly helpless. All I could think about was what was the point of living anymore if I was going to live like this.

At this point, I felt like there was only one option: I had to end it all. If this was what my life would be like, I didn't want it anymore. I was going to kill myself.

*****

One night, I went to the store and bought some liquor. Then, at home, I ordered a pizza from Papa John's and took out my bottle of valium. The plan was simple: I would overdose that night and never wake up again. I would finally eliminate the unknown attacker that had taken over my body. With everything laid out, I was ready to commit suicide when my doorbell rang. I looked at the clock. It was 10 o'clock at night, and I wasn't expecting anyone. I grabbed my cane and hobbled to the door. I opened it to find an elderly lady standing in front of me. She was very petite with delicate features and stood there holding a bible.

I had never seen her before, but she introduced herself as one of the residents in the building and said she had seen me coming and going a lot in ambulances. I will never forget what she said next for the rest of my life.

"God told me to come and check on you."

Those words shook me to my core, and I was actually scared. *God sent her here on the night I was going to commit suicide*! I couldn't believe it. She asked if she could come in, and of course, I let her into my home. She sat with me and asked what was wrong. Her question opened the floodgates of my emotions, and I told her I didn't know. I didn't know, the doctors didn't know, and no one could make me better. She sat quietly and listened to my story.

"Do you believe in God?"

"Yes. Yes, I believe in God."

She pulled out a prayer card and started reciting Psalm 23:

The Lord is my shepherd; I shall not want.

He maketh me to lie down in green pastures: he leadeth me beside the still waters.

He restoreth my soul: he leadeth me in the paths of righteousness for his name's sake.

Yea, though I walk through the valley of the shadow of death, I will fear no evil: for thou art with me; thy rod and thy staff they comfort me.

Do you mind if I pray here with you?" I didn't mind at all. I sat there listening to her words. She told me how God would help me find out what was wrong. He is not going to let me go on like this. She told me to keep looking, to have faith, and to believe.

I will never forget that night. The whole thing was like an out-of-body experience. I was at the lowest point of my life, and it was all over for me. But then this woman, who I had never talked to before, reached out to me and came to my door. I took all this as a sign from God that I was not supposed to kill myself.

God had another plan for me: to find out what was wrong with my health. I needed to have faith that God would put the right doctor on my path. I held on to this faith and restarted my quest to find a doctor who could give me some answers. Again, I found myself in and out of hospitals and private practices.

Each trip was more brutal than the last. At first, I took the train because it was the fastest way to commute from uptown to downtown. But it wasn't long before I couldn't handle the strange way people looked at me. I would be sitting there shaking and twitching, and other passengers would get up, move away, and hold their children tighter.

I tried to make my situation more understandable by wearing more fitted clothing so people could see I wasn't faking the movements. I wore oversized sunglasses to hide my facial twitches and tried to mask my vocal tics and grunts. But it didn't help, and soon, public transport was too embarrassing to bear. I grew more and more ashamed of my state. In the end, I started spending money on cabs and car services to shield myself from the public's gaze.

I saw seven more doctors, each just as confused as the next. I told them that a previous doctor advised me to get the test for Huntington's disease, but they just wouldn't do it. Again, it was the same BS, "You're black, so you can't have it," end of story. They examined me and came up with all kinds of theories. Most of them dismissed my physical symptoms entirely and said it was psychological.

For a time, it seemed like the entire medical community of New York had thrown logic out the window and had gone bonkers. No one had a reasonable, rational answer. I knew it was not all in my head, and that conviction helped me hold on to my faith. God had the right doctor waiting for me. I was so close. I went back online and searched like a woman obsessed, and that's where I found Dr. L.

Dr. L reminded me of the infamous TV doctor, House. He was rational, quirky, and brutally honest. This doctor said whatever was on his mind, threw in a few curses for good measure, and didn't care what anyone thought. He wasn't very popular in his medical circle. Many of his colleagues were also neurologists, and they did not like him. That's not to say he wasn't a good doctor. He just had a very polarizing personality, but that also meant that he did not take any bullshit and would not be swayed by other doctors' opinions. I knew he would give me answers. The first time I walked into his private practice, he was shocked at how badly I was shaking. He and his assistant had to help me walk to the examination room because I was in such a bad state.

"We need to make sure you are not dying!" That was the first thing he said to me. The man was bold but took my symptoms seriously, which was all that mattered.

"What do you mean: *make sure I am not dying*??"

"Well, whatever this is, it's not good."

I told him everything I had been through since moving into my apartment, from my symptoms to the gas leaks and what other doctors said. I didn't leave anything out. He listened and believed me. Do you know what it is like to finally have a medical professional believe you after so many didn't? You are no longer that crazy person who is losing their mind.

His acceptance of my physical state made me feel human again. Dr. L was the one who finally got the test for Huntington's disease done. The results came back, and it confirmed what Dr. C had suspected: I was positive for Huntington's disease.

I should have been relieved to finally have an answer, but this was not the one I wanted. I had been reading up on the disease, and what I had learned was not comforting. There was no cure for Huntington's. Yes, there were management treatments to control the symptoms, but they would not stop my body from degenerating. The symptoms were going to get progressively worse, and my body was going to keep failing. All I had learned was that one day, I would die from it. It was a grim realization.

They say 1 in every 10,000 people has Huntington's, and if you have a family history of the disease, you are more likely to get it. Interestingly, only 10 – 15% of people who are at risk get tested. Before my diagnosis, I would have been surprised by that statistic. Why wouldn't you want to know if you have a genetic disease? But now I understand. No one wants to know how they will die. It is information you can't unlearn. The rest of your life will be dedicated to this disease.

But this genetic test and its subsequent diagnosis was not the end. It also revealed that I had *reduced penetrance* for Huntington's, a mysterious gray area in the realm of this disease. People who are diagnosed with reduced penetrance may or may not develop symptoms. If they do, it will be in the later stages of life, from 65 – 75. There is absolutely no way to predict the outcome of such cases, unlike full penetrance, which always results in the development of symptoms.

But here I am, an exception to all the rules:

1. I am an African American who was never supposed to get Huntington's with the disease.
2. I have reduced penetrance but am showing all the symptoms of someone with full penetrance.
3. I should have started showing symptoms in my older years after my 60s, but it had started in my 30s instead.

None of it made any sense. According to my doctor and the research I continued to do, environmental factors can trigger symptoms. In my case, the two years of continuous natural gas and carbon monoxide exposure pushed my symptoms into effect 30 years before its time.

Now I was angry. It turns out my life was stolen from me. This gas leak was left unchecked by the ineptitude of the gas company and the landlords of my building. Both parties played a part, both were equally guilty, and I wasn't going to stay quiet.

So, in January 2012, I filed a lawsuit against both of them - a lawsuit that would consume the next decade of my life.

Chapter 5: What Is Huntington's Disease?

Let's take a moment away from my story to talk about genetics and its role in Huntington's disease. I think it is essential to understand the science behind this disease because it shows why my situation is unique. Let's start with the basics:

- We have 23 chromosomes inside our cells which are made of a substance called DNA.

- DNA is our blueprint. It tells us how we will grow and what we will look like. It is made of four molecules called bases.

- These bases are adenine (A), cytosine (C), guanine (G), and thymine (T). These repeat over and over again to create long strands of DNA.

- These repeating bases create sequences called genes.

- Each gene codes some specific aspect of our body, and we inherit them from our parents, so we have two copies of each one.

- Each gene has variations known as alleles, with slight differences. Some are dominant, which means they are the ones that express whatever information they have.

This may sound complicated, but the easiest way to understand this concept is with an example, so let's look at the gene that codes eye color.

There are multiple alleles for the eye color gene, such as black, brown, blue, green, and gray. Brown eye color is a dominant allele, so if both of your parents have brown eyes, you will too. If one of your parents has brown eyes, there is at least a 50% chance you will too.

The gene for Huntington's, known as the HD gene, is like the gene for brown eyes. It is dominant. If one of your parents has it, there is at least a 50% chance you will too.

So, what does this HD gene do? Nothing good, it turns out. It is a faulty gene that creates a compound called *huntingtin*, which attacks the brain cells and causes permanent brain damage.

Scientists can tell if this gene is faulty by counting the number of CAG repeats in it. If you have even one HD gene with too many CAG repeats, you will develop Huntington's sometime in your life. There are three stages to this disease, denoted as early, middle, and late, as described below:

EARLY STAGE

Those in the early stages of Huntington's are still quite functional. They can live independently and handle their affairs by themselves. This includes working, driving, managing money, and so on.

At this stage, symptoms are more subtle and harder to pick up, like slight behavioral changes like irritability and depression. Physically, there can be minor involuntary movements, some loss of coordination, and some difficulty concentrating on tasks. In people who don't know they have a faulty HD gene, these symptoms are often misdiagnosed for other conditions.

MIDDLE STAGE

During the middle stages of Huntington's disease, people begin to lose the ability to manage their lives independently. Uncontrollable, jerky movements become more obvious, and general body control is much harder.

Working, driving, or performing household chores at this stage becomes difficult. However, patients can still eat, dress, and attend to personal hygiene with some assistance.

There are often other problems with balance, falling, and weight loss. Cognitively, it becomes harder to problem solve because organizing and sequencing information becomes increasingly difficult.

LATE STAGE
The late stages of Huntington's find the patients bedridden and nonverbal. They need help in every aspect of their life. Some may retain some level of comprehension, but that varies from case to case.

Chorea may be severe, but in most cases, it is replaced by rigidity, twisting (dystonia), and slowness in movements (bradykinesia). It is much harder to diagnose psychiatric symptoms at this stage because communication becomes difficult.

In the medical community, there are two generally accepted rules:

1. If a person has an HD gene with 40 or more CAG repeats, they have full penetrance Huntington's disease.

2. If the HD genes have 26 or fewer CAG repeats, they will NOT get Huntington's disease.

You can see that a range of numbers is not accounted for here: 27 – 39 CAG repeats. This is the gray area I mentioned earlier, called the *reduced penetrance range*. What happens to someone here? Researchers can't say for sure. People here may or may not develop symptoms. Unfortunately, there is no way to know who will and who won't. Still, studies have shown that those who do develop Huntington's get it much later in life, after 60, and with less severity than full penetrance.

According to my genetic test for Huntington's disease, I had 39 CAG repeats. That put me in the reduced penetrance range, which, according to all the research, meant that if I ever got Huntington's, it should NOT be the full-blown symptoms that I was currently experiencing.

If the genetics of Huntington's disease weren't confusing enough, there is also the environmental factor to consider. You may be thinking, *what does the environment have to do with a genetic disease?* This is an understandable question because many of us believe that a *genetic* or *inherited* disease is just something we are born with, end of the story. But this is not always true, especially in the case of Huntington's Disease.

Allow me to introduce you to the famous Venezuela Project[1]. This decades-long medical study has been investigating villages along the shores of Lake Maracaibo in Venezuela since the 1980s because it has one of the highest concentrations of people with Huntington's disease. Worldwide, this disease affects 1 in 10,000, but in this region of Venezuela, it is closer to 1 in 10.

---

[1] (HDF) The US – Venezuela Collaborative Research Project

Over the years, this study has grown to encompass ten generations. That's over 18,000 individuals, some 15,400 who are still alive. Blood and tissue samples from people here helped researchers discover many new things about the disease. They were able to map the HD gene on chromosome 4 in 1983[2] and then discover the CAG repeat mutation in 1993[3].

Researchers also learned that the HD gene can expand as it passes through generations. This means that the number of CAG repeats can increase on its own, which also explains why an estimated 10% of people with Huntington's don't have a family history of the disease.

What's more, external factors can trigger this mutated gene to start making the brain-damaging *huntingtin* compound. There is so much new information now that Huntington's can no longer be classified as an open-and-shut case of "you have the gene, so you have the disease" or "the more CAG – repeats you have, the sooner you will develop the disease."

This is especially true for cases of reduced penetrance. The number of CAG repeats literally tells you nothing about your prognosis. You won't know when symptoms will start showing, nor will you know how severe they will be. Two people can have the same number of CAG repeats in the reduced penetrance range but show completely different symptoms at different ages. As a matter of fact, the Venezuela Project found that in people with reduced penetrance, the CAG repeats only explained the age of onset for about 40% of cases[4].

So what about the remaining 60%? Why were some people showing symptoms earlier than others, even though they had fewer CAG repeats?

---

[2] (Gusella, et al., 1983), [2] (Andrew, et al., 1993) [2] (HDF)

These questions are why researchers believe Huntington's disease is actually a multifactorial disease and external factors can actually trigger the onset. There are hundreds of chemicals and gases listed as carcinogenic and toxic because they can cause genetic mutations. Carbon monoxide is one of them. To say that the gas exposure did not trigger my symptoms would be ignoring a lot of the research available in the world today.

Unfortunately, all this information is not general knowledge. Even more regrettable, it is not even popular medical knowledge. There are still too many doctors in the medical field who follow ancient theories, like Dr. F. When I read articles that say *"Huntington's is most common in Europe and North America,"* I always wonder where these writers get their data to make such claims.

Given the racist history of the healthcare system, I doubt there are any reliable historical medical records about non-white patients. And given ridiculous biases, like *"black people can't have Huntington's,"* the symptoms of our ancestors were either ignored or misdiagnosed.

With incomplete medical data, it is easy to make sweeping statements disregarding entire populations. But it has major consequences because it becomes all the harder for people like me to get an accurate diagnosis and the right treatment.

***

After my diagnosis, it was important to test my parents back home in Cleveland for Huntington's as I inherited the HD gene from at least one of them. Even my siblings needed to get tested because both had a 50 – 50 chance of carrying the faulty gene. My father's test came back normal, but not my mother's. She had precisely the same number as me, 39 CAG repeats. This meant that my mother had reduced penetrance for Huntington's, and I inherited it from her.

Now check this out. Both my mother and I had the same faulty HD gene, and the same number of CAG repeats, 39. So, our HD genes are genetically identical. When my mother was my age, 35, she was completely asymptomatic. She had zero Huntington's related symptoms. Now, at the age of 70, she is starting to show signs of this disease.

Now, look at me. At age 35, I had more aggressive symptoms than my mother at 70. I am taking more medication than she is to manage my condition. I should have also started showing signs in my 70s, not 30 years earlier. Why did my symptoms start sooner? Why are my symptoms so much more severe?

Here, it is no longer about genetics. Here, we have to consider the difference between my mother's life and mine. The most significant factor I see is the environment we lived in. My mother spent her whole life in Cleveland. In contrast, I spent two solid years continuously breathing toxic, poisonous gases in my New York City apartment.

***

None of my siblings got tested when my parents first were because back then, no one really understood this disease. They did not grasp how seriously it could affect the rest of their lives and so brushed it off as no big deal. It was only recently that my sister was tested.

She didn't back then when my parents were because she was in denial. She was ignorant of the disease and didn't want to know anything about it. Unfortunately, her results came back positive for full penetrance Huntington's. It is terrible to learn, but I am not totally surprised by it. The more I educated myself about this disease, the more I realized my sister was always genetically positive. Throughout her life, she dealt with mental health issues, even being diagnosed with bipolar disorder and even schizophrenia.

Many people with Huntington's are often misdiagnosed with such health conditions because many doctors overlook the cognitive effects of Huntington's if they don't see a family history of the disease. I was with her for the whole process, which was difficult to witness. I knew what her future had in store for her, I was going through it myself, and it was a terrible feeling.

My brother doesn't want to get tested and has avoided it so far. But I am afraid he is in the same boat as my sister. Just like her, he has been dealing with mental health issues that I am sure are all misdiagnosed. He is a troubled soul who had many run-ins with the law and problems with alcohol and drug addiction. When I think of him, I often wonder if his behavior could be down to a faulty HD gene.

But there is no way of knowing, and I can't force him to get a test. He avoids me like the plague, and so we are estranged. Maybe he doesn't want to look at me because I could be what his future is like, but this is just my assumption. When there is a disease like Huntington's in the family, it is very difficult for everyone. You can't really blame anyone, yet you are angry at the same time, making it harder to accept the cards you were dealt.

***

I remember watching commercials on TV that would say something along the lines of:

If you lived in a so-and-so area and consumed the water and then developed cancer or Parkinson's, you can claim compensation! Join this class action lawsuit, the people vs. so-and-so.

Parkinson's disease shares many of the same symptoms as Huntington's, to the point that many people with Huntington's are often misdiagnosed with Parkinson's.

What's interesting to note about Parkinson's is that it also has a genetic component, specifically the LRRK2, PARK2, PARK7, PINK1, or SNCA genes[5]. Additionally, 15% of people with Parkinson's have been found to have a family history of the disease. Along with this, there are some other similarities, such as:

- It can appear in a family without any history of Parkinson's, just like Huntington's
- It can be triggered by environmental factors, just like Huntington's

Can you see the point I am trying to make here? I truly believe that if people with Parkinson's or other diseases similar to Huntington's can claim compensation, then so can I. I had just been diagnosed with a condition I would have to treat for the rest of my life. I would need medical care until the very end. This compensation wouldn't cure me, but it would help my future.

But it wasn't just about the money. The gas company needed to know what they did. Society needed to be aware of what was happening around them and that it could happen to them. I had so much evidence on my side, and I knew I had a solid case. But this lawsuit wasn't limited to just the gas company.

I also named all the landlords of my apartment building, Mr. S, Mr. B, and Mr. R. Even though my New York Apartment building changed hands, they were all guilty because they knew about the gas leaks, faulty carbon monoxide meter, and other code violations.

Of course, they pointed the finger at each other. Mr. B and Mr. R said the building was riddled with issues when they bought it.

---

[5] (Cheon, Chan, Kam Yin Chan, & Woo Kim, 2012)

The gas leaks started before it was even in their hands, so Mr. S was accountable. Mr. S said that Mr. B and Mr. R own the building now, so they are responsible for repairing all the issues, regardless of when they started. I wasn't interested in this blame game. In my eyes, both of them were at fault, which is why I named both in the first place. Neither party made an effort, when they owned the building, to resolve the problems promptly. All of them let it drag while I kept breathing in poison.

All of these parties were 100% at fault, not for the disease itself, but for my getting it in my 30s. My genetic test that showed 39 CAG repeats, which is reduced penetrance. I was supposed to start developing symptoms in my late 60s, not three decades before. The extended exposure to the gas leaks had triggered it.

If the landlords had kept the apartment up to code, I would have never been exposed to the toxic gas in the first place. If the gas company had done its job properly and shut the gas completely the first time, my symptoms might not have been aggravated as much as they are now. I would not be dealing with the full-blown symptoms I have today.

Not only that, but their employees, the gas meter readers who were coming every month, never once reported or told me that my meter was illegally installed. I was sitting on a ticking time bomb, and the gas company had turned a blind eye. These people took my life away from me at 35, and they shouldn't be allowed to get away with it. In my opinion, my case was airtight and backed by science. I was ready for court.

Chapter 6: The Court Summons

Taking a case like this to court is not like the movies. You don't just show up with the force of your convictions and give a passionate speech to the jury. There are no *oohs* or *aahs*, rounds of applause or cheers that swell up in the background.

No, it is a long, tiring, complicated experience that can drag on and on for years. In reality, a case has to go through many due processes, from paperwork to preliminary hearings, before it even comes to a jury. There is so much red tape you have to get through, so many technicalities and clauses that it becomes convoluted. It is especially unfair if you can't afford a dedicated legal team.

According to the law, my lawsuit was a toxic tort claim, as explained below:

- A *tort* is for intentional civil wrongs, like personal injuries, damage to property, emotional distress, and defamation.

- A *toxic tort* is a specific type of personal injury lawsuit caused by exposure or contact with a dangerous chemical or environmental substance.

These cases are some of the hardest to win because it is up to the person who is filing, the *plaintiff*, to gather all the evidence, research, and expert testimony that proves every aspect of their case. Any doubt or discrepancy can be enough to derail an entire case. The more plaintiffs there are, i.e., the more people with the same problem, the more likely the case will succeed and get a settlement. These are known as *mass torts* or class *action lawsuits* and are usually the ones you hear about in the news. Some of the most famous toxic tort cases include:

action lawsuits and are usually the ones you hear about in the news. Some of the most famous toxic tort cases include:

- Mesothelioma caused by exposure to asbestos
- Different types of cancer caused by groundwater contamination done by Pacific Gas and Electric Company (PG&E)
- Ovarian cancer from Johnson & Johnson talc powder
- Non-Hodgkin's lymphoma from Roundup weed killer

In all these cases, many people got sick after exposure to the same toxins, which gave their lawsuit weight. The case against PG&E was even turned into the award-winning movie *Erin Brockovich*. In the movie, you can see that the legal team spends most of its time collecting testimony and evidence from residents in the affected area.

Unfortunately, there weren't other people whom I could include in a class action lawsuit. So, mine was going to be exponentially harder. I was all by myself. Every part of my situation was unheard of in the medical community. First, I was never supposed to get Huntington's as an African American. Second, I had reduced penetrance but early onset with full-blown symptoms. Finally, I was exposed to toxic gas and carbon monoxide for two years, which triggered the disease. There was no recorded case like mine in any research paper or medical book, but here I was, and the world needed to know about me. They need to know that I exist.

The first step towards legal justice was finding a personal injury lawyer, i.e., an attorney specializing in toxic tort cases. Like all my searches, I turned to the internet to find someone to help me. Finding a reliable lawyer was just as hard as finding a good doctor. It took time, but I finally found a team I knew would fight for me.

Then, I needed to sit with them and go over the whole story from the beginning to the present day, specifying whom I was suing and why. Precision is key because you can't just go to court and say that *that person did wrong by me.* You need specifics, facts, and dates. This information defines the lawsuit and is what will be sent to the people you are filing against, i.e., the defendants.

I told my legal team everything I have told you so far about my story up to this point. They wrote every word and drilled me for hours to get the right events, dates, and conversations. There were two major threads to my case:

1. The malfunctioning oven in my kitchen led to the discovery of the gas leak
2. My medical history and how my health was steadily deteriorating.

These two threads weaved into each other, and I had to keep the facts straight. Collecting all this information took a considerable time because never forget, I was always extraordinarily sick. Even though my Huntington's test results had not come back, I still needed to take medication to control the symptoms I was exhibiting, each with its own side effects.

Commuting to the offices and then to court was a nightmare for me. My illness was clearly visible. I was using a walker, shaking and twitching constantly. As I look back at that time, I think someone with so many problems should not be able to get out of bed. But again, here I was. Looking back, it was the sheer power of will that kept me going.

On January 16, 2012, the gas company and the landlords were served my official complaints, i.e., the summons. That document was a legal notice that covered all my complaints, from their negligence to reckless behavior concerning the gas stove and gas lines. It was a detailed notice with over thirty points of action. Specific allegations included:

> *The defendants had the "non-delegable duty" to "own, operate, manage and maintain the premise in compliance with the laws, statutes, and regulations of the State of New York" and "equip the plaintiff's apartment with appropriate meters, piping, and valves as we as with the proper functional smoke and carbon monoxide detectors capable of warning the plaintiff and other of the presence of carbon monoxide in or about the premise."*

Here, *"non-delegable"* means the gas company and the landlord were solely responsible for their duties and could not transfer that to someone. Just because they told someone else to deal with it does not mean they can put their heads under the sand.

I made it a point to mention that these people were also responsible for the carbon monoxide detectors. I would have moved out of that apartment sooner if I had known about the leaks. So, there is a strong possibility that my symptoms would not have been as aggravated.

> *"The defendants were negligent in installing, maintaining, and repairing the gas oven in an improper manner."*

> *The gas company "undertook repairs and corrective measures in the plaintiff's apartment upon which the plaintiff relied, and that said repairs or actions were done in a negligent manner, which caused and allowed the plaintiff to remain in the apartment despite the ongoing and dangerous conditions."*

Here, I specified that the gas company failed to do the repairs properly, and I was completely unaware of their failure.

All my symptoms started after I moved into that apartment. Then, when I lost my job because of the back injury, I spent more time in my apartment and got sicker. This effect is what connects the gas leaks to my condition.

In the summons, I named the actions of the gas company and landlords' *ultra-hazardous activity* and that I was the only person who suffered for it. Their neglect didn't hurt them. It hurt me. And not just in the short term but until the day I die.

When I sat with my lawyers, they documented all my symptoms, and let me tell you, it was not short. I had been to over 20 doctors multiple times. My medical file was an encyclopedia filled with doctor's exams corroborating my symptoms.

There was no exaggeration or "massaging the truth." I just listed word for word exactly what I was dealing with, and it was not a short list! My health issues covered over 75 different symptoms and disabilities. Over six pages long, here are just a few of the symptoms from my case:

1. Carbon monoxide and methane poisoning
2. Triggering of Huntington's disease
3. Permanent brain damage leading to cognitive, motor, and memory deficiencies and disabilities
    - foci of t2 and flair signal hyper-intensities within the white matter of the brain

- foci of abnormal signal intensity within the subcortical regions of the frontal operculum bilaterally
   - demyelination of the white matter of the brain
   - abnormal signal intensity within the inferior portion of the brain of the right caudate nucleus
4. Chorea and chorea movement disorder
   - thrusting movements of the trunk
   - facial and eye twitching
   - involuntary grunting
   - muscle twitching of the back, the arms and legs, hands and feet
   - impaired gait and balance
5. severe pain, agony, and suffering
6. speech disturbances
7. Slurred speech
8. Abdominal contractions
9. Chest pain
10. Fatigue and weakness
11. Dizziness and vertigo
12. respiratory difficulties
13. nausea
14. nosebleeds
15. hair loss
16. blurred vision
17. sleep disturbance
18. mental anguish
   - anxiety and agitation, suicidal thoughts
   - emotional distress and suffering
   - severe depression

- anxiety and panic attacks

19. risk of developing Parkinson's, cancer

20. Loss of enjoyment of life and shortened life span.

After this legal notice was delivered to the defendants, I received my Huntington's Test results in the next month on February 28, 2012, my birthday.

What a way to welcome my thirty-seventh year on this Earth. In black and white, I finally had the answer to all my problems. Even before I had this paper in my hands, I had mentally prepared myself for it. I had been researching online to learn more about it, but all that preparation didn't help.

There was no consolation because all it confirmed was that all my symptoms were permanent and would get worse as I got older, leading to my death one day. I was officially handicapped and would never be able to live unassisted again. I would face so many issues, such as:

- Inability to work and be financially capable
- Inability to perform normal daily activities
- Inability to become pregnant and carry a fetus to term
- Inability to adopt a child
- Inability to maintain relationships and follow medical treatment
- The necessity of being on medications for the remainder of my life
- The necessity of undergoing speech, physical, occupational, and cognitive therapy
- need for daily assistance to ensure personal safety, daily living, and medical treatment
- The necessity of living in a handicapped-equipped apartment

I won't pretend like these results didn't leave me bitter. That birthday was a dark day for me. I could not see a happy future for myself.

I hope by now, you can understand that this case was not just some ploy for revenge or to punish my perpetrators. No, there was no satisfaction in any of it. I was suffering every step of the way. The monetary compensation I demanded was not about making the defendants *suffer*. It was about holding them responsible by taking into account all the expenses I would incur over the span of my, albeit limited, life. These were not "normal" expenses because they also include the medical requirements I require to function at the most basic level, such as:

- Future physician expenses
- Future medical supply expenses
- Future diagnostic expenses, such as blood tests, biopsies, x-rays, MRIs, and CT scans
- Future hospitalizations
- Future full-time nurse expenses
- Future therapeutic expenses, such as physical therapy

Not to mention the loss of future earnings. This all adds up. Understand, what I was asking for wasn't so I could buy a mansion in the country or go on a fancy vacation, and we didn't just throw out a random amount.

My legal team hired an economist to crunch the numbers. This person took into account all these expenses and calculated the amount I would need to survive the remainder of my years without being a burden to anyone. And if anyone should pay me, it should be the people who put me in this condition first.

Around the time the summons was sent, two major changes took place in my life. First, I moved out of my apartment, and second, my treatment for the now-confirmed Huntington's began. The gas company claimed they had fixed all the gas leaks. Still, I wasn't going to spend another minute in that apartment and -move out the first opportunity I got.

The apartment I moved into was a small studio in Midtown. It was tiny compared to all the space I had before. You walked into a single room, and everything was in front of you. It was so small that I didn't have enough space for my things, so I either put them in storage or sold them on Craigslist. Given my medical condition, living in a smaller space probably made sense, but I didn't like it. I felt closed in, cramped, with no room to breathe. The building's inhabitants were far more multicultural, with people from around the world. I made friends with some of them, but for the most part, I kept to myself.

Midtown was so different from Uptown. For one, Times Square is right there, and it is one of the busiest parts of Manhattan. There is so much happening and so many people coming and going. The sheer volume of people, street performers, and whatnot, for the first time in a while, I didn't stand out, and it was a welcomed change. The best part about this area was there was plenty of public transport so I could get where I needed to be much faster and more conveniently. Of course, most of my travels were to doctors, the first being Dr. L. He took charge of my treatment plan and immediately prescribed benazine. This drug would decrease my body's uncontrolled, jerky movements, medically known as chorea. He also prescribed painkillers for the constant pain in my arms and legs.

Known as neuropathy, it had nothing to do with Huntington's but was, in fact, due to the gas poisoning in the apartment. Those toxic fumes had damaged the nerve endings in my limbs so badly that nothing could be done to fix them. All Dr. L could do was dull the pain.

As Dr. L continued to examine my health and progress, he kept adjusting my medications, adding new ones, removing others, and adjusting dosages to get to a place where most of my symptoms were managed. I also had to have physical and speech therapy to exercise and regain some control of my body.

Reading all this might make it sound like my quality of life changed drastically, but nothing improved overnight. There was so much trial and error with the medications that it was more like a bumpy road filled with twists and setbacks. Every time a drug or dosage was changed, there would be adjustment periods of either nothing happening or symptoms worsening.

You know, the human body is strange but fascinating like that. Anything the immune system perceives as foreign, it attacks, even if it is a life-saving drug. What ends up happening is that your body develops a resistance to the drug and that medicine becomes ineffective. So doctors have to stay one step ahead and make alterations so your body does develop this drug resistance. Despite taking medication, I was still dealing with symptoms that could not be cured. My sense of balance and space were still unreliable. I would fall repeatedly, and each fall required a trip to the ER. I was assigned a social worker to help me live normally because I could not manage my life on my own.

Another essential but demanding part of my treatment was counseling. I started regularly seeing a psychologist and psychiatrist who closely watched my mental and emotional state. Talking to a psychologist helped highlight the problems, like anxiety and depression, and the prescribed medication, like Prozac, helped alleviate them.

My days were a blur of trips to the ER, doctors' appointments, and therapy sessions. It was all so overwhelming. There was so much going on, and it felt like every part of my being was being tested and analyzed. Before the year was over, I was taking a cocktail of drugs, but none to cure myself. None of the medicines could even slow down the disease. They were just bandages to mask the symptoms. I knew it and still felt sick.

With my diagnosis and the start of treatment in 2012, I had reached a turning point in my health, but I didn't feel hopeful. It seemed to me like there was no light at the end of the tunnel, and treating this disease would be all my life was going to be about.

I suffered from depression that was so severe I had to be hospitalized for it. It wasn't just that I felt sad. The medications also played a part. Take my chorea medication, benazine. While it was reducing the movements, it affected my brain's chemical balance, depleting dopamine and serotonin, two of our natural "feel good" hormones. This medication fed my depression, and I was drowning in feeling like I was fighting a losing battle. What was the point of it all if Huntington's would beat me in the end?

But I will say there was some contentment in knowing what exactly was wrong with me. After months of running around the city visiting incompetent doctor after doctor, I was grateful for the clarity. That was infinitely better than being in the dark. As I was trying to figure out the next step for my health, the answer from the defendants arrived.

Chapter 7: The Defendants' Answer

On April 30th, 2012, four months after receiving my complaint, the defendants replied to my claims. In their answer, they denied everything from my allegations to my existence. I would have been offended, but I had enough experience as a paralegal to know this is a classic defense response, so I was not surprised.

Very rarely do defendants in any kind of case admit to wrongdoing. And in toxic tort cases, they will fight tooth and nail to absolve themselves of ever harming the plaintiff. A defense team's first response is to act like they have no clue about what is going on, and then they work day and night to prove that the plaintiff is responsible for their own misfortune.

So naturally, neither the gas company nor the landlords admitted they did anything wrong. My legal team knew this, as did I. Among the many denials in their answer, here is a direct quote of what they had to say about the *injuries* (my medical condition):

"The injuries were sustained while they [the plaintiff] were involved in an activity into which they had entered knowing full well the hazards thereof and the inherent risk incident to such activity."

"The risks and dangers, if any, were open, obvious, notorious, and apparent."

All this legal jargon essentially states that if there was anything hazardous in the apartment, I was well aware of it. In other words, I knew about the gas leaks and willingly sat in that apartment for as long as I did despite the hazard to my health.

This classic victim blaming is very common in toxic tort cases. So, again, it was expected. Other lines of defense from their answer included:

"The plaintiff's injuries, if any, were caused by the intervening acts of third parties unrelated to this answering defendant,"

"The answering defendant did not owe the plaintiff any of the duties alleged in the lawsuit."

"The answering defendant was without notice of any of the purported conditions alleged in this complaint."

Here, the defendants (the gas company and landlords) claim they are in no way responsible for anything that happened to me in that apartment, and someone else should be held accountable. Additionally, they stated they had no obligations toward me and had no clue that I was going through any of the medical issues I had listed in my lawsuit.

The defendants also cautioned that the amount I pursued should be reduced if I did win my case. According to them, I could claim other monetary benefits like insurance, social security, worker's compensation, or employee benefit programs. They believed they were liable for 50% at most.

In their own eyes, the defendants were completely innocent. The gas company believed they only had one job: to come in and take a meter reading, while the landlords were only supposed to collect the rent. Apparently, all the housing codes listed by the state of New York didn't apply to either.

With this answer, the defense team also sent a list of questions. My lawsuit was in its discovery phase, and the defense had to build a case. So they needed to know everything I did to argue against it. I was more than ready to reply back. Having been through so much, I wanted the defendants to know every detail of how they made my health so much worse.

My answers to their questions were sent on February 13th, 2013, almost a year later, which I know seems like a long time. But there are several reasons why, the most significant being the general state of the legal system in this country. So many cases are being processed simultaneously and a severely limited number of resources that it forms a bottleneck, delaying everything.

Other than the inherent delays of the courts, I was also in the middle of moving to a new apartment and starting my Huntington's therapy in the hopes of returning some order to my life. Then, of course, my legal team had to verify all the information I supplied. All of these factors just slowed my case down further.

Coming back to this document, officially known as a Bill of Particulars, I responded to each of the defense team's questions, which were extensive. They asked for everything from my date of birth and social security number to the names and addresses of all the New York doctors I visited.

As for questions related to the gas leaks, I went into excruciating detail explaining how the leaks were discovered and all the failures of the landlords and gas company, including:

- The problems I had with my stove
- My complaints to the landlords
- The super coming in again and again to fix it
- The landlords' various attempts to solve the gas problems
- The gas company's multiple visits and their inability to lock the gas meter properly

My attorneys used precise language to specify every point where the defendants were at fault, closing any possible loopholes for them to slip out. Salient points from my response are as follows:

1. Continuous gas exposure from August 1st, 2009 until July 2011
2. The incorrect encasement of the gas meter in the wall and the defendants (including their agents, servants, and employees) not properly maintaining, monitoring, or repairing it or any of the gas lines running through the apartment
3. The failure of the gas company to correct the deficiencies and defects in the gas service
4. The failure of the gas company to properly shut off, lock, cap, or plug the gas line on February 24th, 2011
5. The failures of the gas company to rectify its mistake until July 2011, five months later.
6. The violation of New York City Administrative Code sections 27-2046.1, 27-2046.2, and 27-2045 against the landlords for failing to maintain operational carbon monoxide and smoke detectors.
7. An unresolved carbon monoxide detector violation against the landlords for a faulty one
8. The failure of the landlords to promptly hire a licensed plumber or contractor to repair the defects in the apartment
9. The disregard of the landlords who allowed illegal renovation inside the apartment.
10. The carelessness of the landlords who told me to open the windows and not call the gas company.

As far as reckless and negligent behavior go, there is no question that the gas company and landlords were running wild. It is wrong not to inform prospective tenants about all the housing violations in an apartment building. The landlord's behavior is particularly upsetting. He never told me about any of them. If I had known the building had faulty carbon monoxide detectors or gas pipe issues, I would have thought twice before signing the lease.

I think one of the reasons none of the other tenants in the apartment ever complained about anything before was because of immigration issues. As I mentioned earlier, this apartment was in Washington Heights, Washington Heights, a location with a predominant Dominican population. I am sure there was a fair share of illegal residents who did not want to draw the attention of the authorities. That would also explain why the landlord was so angry when I called the gas company in the first place. Who knows what kind of agreements he had with the other residents.

It's also worth mentioning that this particular gas company has had many problems over the years. Currently, it is facing several legal issues as it failed to maintain gas supply and lines throughout the city. These problems were bound to happen because infrastructure needs to be taken care of regularly. It can't last a hundred years and function properly on a prayer. This gas company is now known for its negligence, which has finally caught up with it almost ten years later. But my case was far from over, and until this point, I was a pest it needed to get rid of.

After my team sent the Bill of Particulars in 2013, my case faced even more delays. For one, the gas company changed law firms. My attorneys received two notices about these changes in June and July of the same year. Now, different law firms represented the separate entities within the gas company. Think of it like a head office and its subsidiaries. The top management was basically saying *we had nothing to do with your gas problems because we didn't know anything, so deal with our branch in your area.* This just shows how far the company was willing to go to avoid being held responsible.

As for the landlords, they hired a lawyer in November 2013, right at the end of the year. I don't know why they took so long to hire one. Maybe it was a financial issue, or perhaps they hoped I would drop the case. I can't say. I know no one wants to get involved in a legal matter, which may be why they hesitated.

But these changes and delays are never welcomed because there is so much paperwork and due process when cases change hands. It's like more detours on an already long journey. New law firms don't trust anything an old one gives them. They have to go through all the information before deciding if they need more information or are ready to move forward. Like everything in life, it keeps piling up, so it took another few years before the depositions could begin.

Chapter 8: The Depositions

The depositions for my lawsuit didn't start until 2015, three years after I first filed.

A deposition is when the lawyers take the testimony of a witness outside of court and use it to build their case. Again, it is part of the discovery phase, and the information gathered is rarely used in the actual trial. The person who has to answer the lawyers' questions is called the deponent. Every word said, from questions to comments, is transcribed for the record.

Even though a deposition is not taken in court, it is still done under oath, and the deponent is expected to be honest. Lying under oath is a serious offense and is called perjury. You can be fined, put on probation, and even sentenced to jail if you commit perjury.

Despite being a straightforward process, the stakes are high, making it a nerve-wracking experience. You must keep all your facts in order and answer whatever the lawyer asks. And let me tell you, they can ask you about anything you have ever said or done. Not only that but anything you have ever posted online can be brought to light, making it an extremely stressful situation.

Some lawyers purposely make this process more difficult than it needs to be in an attempt to trap you. They word their questions in such a complicated way that you get confused and say something you didn't mean to. Other times, they ask unfair, offensive questions to make you emotional, so, again, you say something they can hold against you.

That is why it is important to go into a deposition mentally prepared and remain calm. The key is to pay attention to what is being asked and to answer as succinctly as possible. Of course, like all things, this is easier said than done.

Another stress-inducing part of these depositions is both sides can call anyone they deem relevant to a case. And when I say anyone, I mean anyone, from your mother to your ex-boyfriend. In other words, lawsuits can get dirty pretty quickly, and if either side gets any information that can shake you, they will use it against you.

In my case, the defendants' lawyers wanted every shred of information about me and everyone around me. They had no limits or boundaries, asking for my family's medical records and all the known contacts I had in the city. They weren't even trying to prove or disprove my claim. They didn't care about the gas leaks or who was responsible. Instead, they were more interested in attacking my character, health, and way of life.

It didn't help that going to court was a sheer nightmare task for me. I was extraordinarily sick, shaking, and suffering. My illness was clearly visible, so no one could say I was faking an illness. Looking back, it was the pure desire for justice that got me out of bed and moving forward. But my current state was not enough for the defense lawyers and they asked every question they could about my medical history in an attempt to pin a past illness on my present conditions. The lawyers inquired about every flu, fever, and sore throat I ever had before moving to New York as well as my health while living in the city. Then, they kept asking about alcohol and drug use, wording questions differently to see if they could catch a lie. They thought they could get their clients off the hook if they pinned my issues on something drug-related.

This line of attack was an obvious choice. It's so easy to put the *drug addict* label on a black person because of the substance abuse problems within the African-American community. But here's the issue: drug and alcohol abuse is not exclusive to a single ethnicity and is prevalent across many. However, people of color suffer the most from stereotyping, and even the most innocent are accused of being an addict without question. This mentality takes me back to my ER visits before my Huntington's diagnosis. When I used to come in shaking, the staff always tried to push the same drug narrative on me instead of doing a proper examination.

I am positive I showed clear signs of carbon monoxide and natural gas poisoning in those days, but their racism wouldn't let them see it. Instead, the ER staff was so sure I was *on* something they didn't bother to check for anything else. I wasn't going to stand for the same treatment during my deposition. There was no way I would let these lawyers pin the same clichéd story on me, not after the rollercoaster I had been on.

By this point, I had started my management treatment for Huntington's, taking a variety of medications that my body was still adjusting to. My involuntary movements and shaking (choreatic movements) were constant, and the anxiety of the deposition seemed to make it worse. Despite having the truth on my side, the entire ordeal was so stressful. I am thankful that my mind and memory were not clouded by the medications, and I could tell my story accurately.

I answered all their accusatory questions concisely and consistently denied all their substance abuse allegations. As the drug angle wasn't working for the defense, they switched gears and started questioning my character. Now, they were asking about my lifestyle and how many boyfriends I had in the past. They wanted to know how I could just move to New York to live with a man. It was unbelievable. None of this was relevant to my claim in the slightest.

The truth of the matter is that anything before 2009 was none of their business. They had no right to pry into such personal topics. But this was not the first time the defense crossed a line. They even called my ex, Andrew, asking him if I would sort things outside of court. I am still appalled by their nerve and how they violated my privacy.

I'm sure those lawyers even went to the doctors I listed in my lawsuit. Not only to check if they existed but to see if I actually went to them. Who knows what information was passed between the lawyers and the doctors. As I said, they were desperate to find something against me or catch a lie because people lie, even under oath.

Speaking of liars, my landlord, Mr. S, was also called in during the depositions. I wasn't present during his questioning but was given a copy of his transcript. It's quite a journey to read. It starts with the lawyers asking him about his background as a landlord, and it turns out Mr. S had been renting out spaces throughout his lifetime. As I read his replies explaining his 30 years as a property owner, I realized that this person must have been aware of a landlord's responsibilities, housing codes, and violation laws in the city.

However, when he purchased the apartment building in question, he did it blindly without thoroughly inspecting the property. In his own words, he *went around and saw the building with his own eyes* but never checked inside any of the apartments, their appliances, or utility pipes, such as the gas lines.

He also claims he put a lawyer in charge of inspections, who gave him the *green light* without checking for open building violations. At the same time, he admitted the previous owner said they would clear up the previous violations. Do you see the contradiction here? He's admitting and denying knowing anything about open violations.

My lawyers asked him about my apartment, and Mr. S stated he had never been inside before I moved in. Even when the previous tenants moved out, he never went upstairs to check the apartment and just sent painters to put a coat of fresh paint on the walls. Mr. S, with his 30 years of rental experience, must have been the first landlord in the history of New York renting who doesn't check how tenants leave apartments.

I find this exceptionally unusual because landlords take security deposits when they lease apartments. That way, if a tenant damages it in any way, they can withhold the deposit. Experienced landlords always check vacated apartments, even for the smallest holes in the wall. If they can't inspect it in person, they hire someone to check it. Moving on, Mr. S acknowledged the presence of Mr. J, the superintendent of the building. He admitted that he would regularly send Mr. J to apartments to deal with tenants' issues but confessed that Mr. J was not a qualified or certified plumber or electrician.

Honestly, I was shocked the first time I read this. It sent me back to those months of frustration and Mr. S repeatedly sending someone who didn't know how to fix the gas and stove problems. It baffles me how Mr. S could do this in good conscience just to save a buck or two. Mr. S also claims that I was the only tenant who complained about gas problems the entire time he owned the building.

My lawyers asked him a series of questions about natural gas that I believe should be highlighted. They are given below, directly quoted from the transcript:

Q. As a landlord, do you agree or disagree that one should use reasonable care in the handling and distribution of natural gas?

A. I don't understand.

Q Do you agree that natural gas can be a dangerous substance?

A. Yes

Q. In your experience as a landlord, do you have an understanding of whether or not natural gas can be explosive in character?

A. I have. I know it's explosive.

Q. Do you have, as a landlord, an understanding of whether natural gas has a tendency to escape and disperse into the environment?

A. Yes, it has.

Q. As a landlord, do you have an understanding as to whether or not leaking gas in a building is a dangerous condition?

A. Yes, it is dangerous

Q. As a landlord, do you view a landlord as having an obligation to prevent the escape of gas within buildings that you own?

A. Yes.

Q. As the landlord, do you have an understanding of who has an obligation to maintain the pipes and lines within a building that you own carrying gas from the meter to an appliance?

A. It is the landlord's responsibility.

Q. Do you know what natural gas smells like?

A. Yes.

Q. Did you ever smell the scent of natural gas at [redacted: address of the apartment]?

A. No.

When I read these answers, I can't help but go back to all the times I told Mr. S and Mr. J about the gas leak in my apartment. I hounded them on the phone and in person for days, but they never took serious action. I used to think maybe Mr. S just doesn't know how dangerous natural gas is, but his deposition tells a different tale.

Mr. S knew full well how perilous my situation was. When thoughts like this flood my mind, they create a domino effect, and I start to relive all those traumatic events. Then I start questioning my life, and all these *what-if scenarios* pop into my head. *What if we had checked for leaks sooner? What if they fixed it sooner? What if I had never been exposed for so long?*

I have done a great deal of emotional healing over the years. I have come to terms with my medical condition, but I would be lying if I said something as trivial, *let bygones be bygones*. To this day, I truly believe that if Mr. S had addressed my concerns when I first made them, the gas exposure would not have triggered the onset of my Huntington's disease so soon.

***

Coming back to the deposition transcript, Mr. S acknowledged that he had met me before I rented the apartment and accompanied me upstairs to view it. He also admits to viewing the apartment once or twice before with other potential tenants. Again, he contradicts his earlier statement of never being inside my apartment before I moved in.

Then he goes on to state that he did, in fact, check the apartment's condition when the previous tenants left, even though he had said the opposite earlier. No matter how much Mr. S tried to deny it, it is obvious that at some point before I moved in, Mr. S walked around my apartment and went into the kitchen area. He would have noticed the renovations, and the gas meter was encased in the wall.

But remember, Mr. S was trying to wash his hands of all wrongdoing, so here are a few other things he denied any knowledge of:

- Where the gas meter was in my apartment
- Where the gas meters were in any of the apartments
- What a gas meter even looked like

Even when my lawyers showed Mr. S photos from my kitchen, such as the stove, cabinetry, and gas meter. Mr. S denied seeing any of these items before. He couldn't identify the gas meter in the photo, alleging he had never seen one before. He also denied having any kitchen renovation or cabinetry work done in the apartment while he was the landlord.

Then, the questioning moved on to the carbon monoxide detectors in my apartment. The following is directly quoted from the transcript:

Q. Do you know whether apartment four had a carbon monoxide detector in the apartment?

A. I don't know.

*Q. **Do you know whether a carbon monoxide detector is required under the building code?***

A. Yes, it is required.

*Q. **Did Ms. Allen ever inform you at any point in the summer of 2010 that the carbon monoxide detector in apartment [redacted] had gone off?***

A. Not to my knowledge.

*Q. **Separate and apart from the summer of 2010, do you recall any conversation with Ms. Allen at any time regarding a carbon monoxide detector having gone off?***

A. No.

If you recall, in the earlier chapters, I mentioned my carbon monoxide detector went off while I lived there, and Mr. S said it was a false alarm. The same man was now denying it ever happened. My lawyers even showed him documentation of a previous violation for a faulty carbon monoxide detector in another apartment, filed during his time as a landlord. Mr. S took it, looked it over, and simply said *I don't recall.*

This landlord thought there were no records of my interactions with him. He thought it was essentially my word against his so he could give his version of the truth. And Mr. S really gave a different story when he related the events surrounding the gas leaks. According to Mr. S's reality, one day, I called him complaining about a gas smell in my apartment. He told me to check the pilot lamp on my stove to see if gas was going into my stove. However, I couldn't find it, so he came to my apartment to help. Unfortunately, he couldn't find the pilot lamp either and didn't know where the smell was coming from. Then, in Mr. S's own words, as written in the deposition transcript:

"She asked me," Should we call [Mr. J]?" and I said, "No, don't call [Mr. J]. It's not the job of [Mr. J]. I am going to get the experts to solve the problem for you. We don't call [Mr. J]at all. It's not his jurisdiction.""

Well, isn't that interesting? Mr. S claims he got an expert immediately and never told the unqualified super to get involved. He also goes on to claim he made every effort to solve my problem and denied ever stopping me from calling the gas company. In fact, he says calling the gas company was the right thing to do because they were the only ones who could solve the problem correctly.

As frustrating as it is to read, I can't help but laugh at his boldness to lie so openly and on record. He really thought he could say whatever he wanted. But like I keep saying, *or so he thought*. It is important to understand our legal system is based on the presence of evidence. Without the cold hard facts, you have nothing to support your case. Evidence can save an innocent person from being wrongly punished. On the other hand, a lack of it can let a guilty person get away.

I know the value of evidence not only because I was a paralegal but because I am a person of color. Unfortunately, my word will always carry less weight in court. Our legal system is also plagued by the same systemic racism that runs deep in our nation, and no one can deny it. Time and time again, I have seen people of color being tried unfairly and handed such severe punishments while white people facing similar accusations are treated so much more leniently.

So trust me when I say I know the importance of having a record and keeping receipts. That is why I made it a point to record every single one of my interactions with the landlord, the super, and any technician who walked through my door. My pocket recorder was always with me, so I have such a clear record of everything that happened. Mr. S may think he can say whatever he wants, but I have the proof that he was lying:

- He was the one who sent the super the first time.
- He was the one who kept sending the super.
- He was the one who delayed calling an expert.
- He was the one who told me not to call the gas company.

My lawyers knew I had recorded all my interactions with him and made sure he answered all related questions. You see, it was no longer a case of his word against mine. It was now his word against his own.

Chapter 9: A Change of Outlook

Legal cases are exhausting experiences even for the healthiest person. So, you can imagine how exceptionally draining this whole process was for me. My emotional state was at an all-time low, and I was depressed all the time.

For the first half of that year, there was an ever-present dark cloud over my head that just made everything seem so hopeless. The only thing that kept me going was the need for justice. And let me tell you, this motivation was in no way positive because there was no joy in winning. Back then, my brain was stuck in this vicious cycle of thinking I would always be sick no matter what, win or lose. Winning would not heal my body, and I would never get better because HD is a degenerative disease with no cure.

This is such a terrible mindset to be in because it leaves you in a dark, dangerous headspace. But at that time, it seemed like nothing could stop bitter thoughts from invading my mind, and for the longest time, I felt helpless, consumed by the belief that my disease was all I had in my life.

But then, in June 2013, I decided to go to a Huntington's convention at the suggestion of my doctors. They said it would be a good place to learn more about my condition, but honestly, I wasn't expecting much. As I mentioned, I was so dejected that I couldn't see any light at the end of my tunnel. But thank God I went because I consider that convention a turning point in my life. This particular event was organized by the Huntington's Disease Society of America (HDSA), a nonprofit advocacy organization for people with Huntington's Disease.

I find the HDSA's story beautiful and truly inspiring. It started over 50 years ago in 1967 with one woman, Marjorie Guthrie, who decided to stand up and bring awareness to the disease that had taken over her husband, Woody Guthrie, and was a threat to her three children.

Woody Guthrie was a famous American folk singer best known for his song, *This Land is Your Land*, a classic that practically everyone sang in school. As is the case with many Huntington's patients, Woody was misdiagnosed several times when his health started to decline. It wasn't until years later that doctors discovered that he was suffering from Huntington's. As Marjorie watched the disease take apart her husband, she realized there had to be other families in the country going through the same thing. Her empathy led her to place ads in newspapers to find them. Even when her husband passed away in 1967, she didn't stop connecting with others and eventually built what is now known as HDSA.

Since then, the HDSA has grown into a massive organization that raises funds and sponsors research and clinical trials, all in the quest to find better treatments for Huntington's disease. The HDSA also keeps families connected, holding annual conferences where HD patients and their families can come together and meet each other, health providers, and researchers.

The one I attended that year was held in Jacksonville, Florida, and it was an eye-opening, life-changing experience. There were over a thousand people from all parts of the country, and I met many HD patients in different stages of the disease. I even got to sit down with some of them and listen to their stories as I shared mine.

Meeting and talking to people who are in the same situation as you and can relate to the way you feel is an incredibly uplifting feeling. Suddenly, I didn't feel so alone anymore. For the first time since my health had started to decline, there was the tiniest shred of hope and a glimmer of a possible future beyond HD. While I learned a lot about my condition at that convention, the knowledge I gained wasn't even the best part. The real victory was connecting with a person I now consider a steadfast friend. Here, I will call Sarah.

Sarah is six years younger than me and also has Huntington's. However, when I met her at the convention all those years ago, she was asymptomatic. Now, she is in her 40s and has only started to show symptoms. Over the years, Sarah has become closer to me than my family. We talk every single day, keeping each other updated on our progress and what is happening in our lives. The fact that she also has HD makes it so much easier for me to share my bad days. She instantly understands me and knows what to say to keep me looking forward. I am so grateful to have her support as I navigate my life.

Interestingly, our health condition isn't the only thing we share. We also share a birthday month! I will always find it amusing that her birthday is February 26th, and mine is the 28th. What were the chances of that? It is funny where life takes you and the people you meet along the way. Take Sarah, for example. Who would have thought my disease would lead me to this person who would become such an irreplaceable presence in my life?

Another significant part of this HD convention was meeting another black family who had flown in from the West Coast. Apart from me, they were the only other African Americans with the HD gene at that convention. Can you believe it? We were the only black people in this sea of patients from across the country. As extraordinary as that was, I felt relief seeing another face like mine. In a way, it was like validation that, yes, black people can get Huntington's disease even if there are still doctors who still say they can't.

This convention taught me an important lesson about humans in general: we are exceptionally social creatures. We will always search for others like us because we find hope and strength in them. When we lose confidence, we turn to our people, who support and pull us up. There is no medicine stronger than the care and compassion of others.

Participating in this convention strongly affected me. I stopped feeling so hopeless and started to see things differently. Of course, I had a genetic condition that had already taken a great deal from me, but it had not taken everything. Not yet, anyway.

One thing was certain: I would never achieve anything more in my life if I continued to sit and wallow in my grief. Seeing all these people at this convention showed me I could still have a life. Obviously, it wouldn't be what I pictured when I first moved to New York, but it could still be fulfilling. I could still find happiness and meaning in my existence.

I would be lying if I said I held on to this newfound positivity and never wavered because I had my dips in faith. The slightest issue or any slip or fall would land me in the ER, and there were many because HD affected my perception and balance.

I was prone to accidents and constantly being hospitalized for one thing or another. Keeping a positive outlook while I lay in a hospital bed for days on end was hard, and it didn't help that my legal case was still dragging on with no end in sight.

But somewhere in all of this, I made a decision. While it was inevitable that Huntington's would take control of all of me one day, and there wasn't much I could do for my body, I could still fight for my mind. So until that day came, I was going to hold on to as much of my cognitive ability as possible, and for me, the best way to do that was to go back to school.

In 2015, I enrolled for an associate's degree in Public Affairs at Empire State College, a school close to my place in Times Square, almost within walking distance. Studying at this college gave me a chance to take my mind off my health and focus on something new. Despite all that had happened to me, I was a civil servant at heart and still wanted to be part of the public service world. Huntington's may never let me work again, but I could not change who I was or stop me from learning more about what I loved.

Studying Public Affairs for the next few years allowed me to lose myself in a subject matter that had nothing to do with my health, and it was like a sweet mental release. Life wasn't just about doctors' appointments and medicines anymore. There were books I needed to read, topics I needed to research, and reports I needed to write. All these micro-goals I needed to achieve gave me a sense of purpose, and I felt like I was doing something again.

Given how Huntington's affects a person's memory and comprehension skills, many assumed I wouldn't be able to cope with the demands of returning to school and would eventually have to drop out.

But I wasn't going to give up that readily. As I said, I found purpose in life again, so I took it day by day, focusing on one task at a time. There were definitely some days that were harder than others, but I always managed to find a way through. In 2017, against all the odds, I graduated with my Associate's Degree. An achievement I am extremely proud of. The fact that I was able to keep studying and that I enjoyed it, I decided to keep going. I went back to Empire State College, and this time, I enrolled in the Bachelor in Public Affairs program.

This course continued to build on the knowledge I had acquired during my associated degrees and was just as demanding, if not more. Nevertheless, I was determined and somehow made time between my therapy sessions and hospital visits to study. Again, people told me I won't be able to complete this degree. Even my doctors thought it would be difficult, but I was never one to believe what doctors said anyway.

For all our frailty and weaknesses, humans can be quite resilient. In the face of all these obstacles, I developed this stubbornness that just won't accept anything else. I pushed myself and am even prouder to say that I completed my bachelor's and graduated in 2022.

***

While studying, my legal battle was still going on in the background. Until March 2016, the gas company was not ready to move to the next stage before a judge. In fact, that month, we found out that they had filed a countersuit against the plumbing company in charge of the repairs. According to the gas company, they didn't do anything wrong because it wasn't their responsibility to make the repairs.

They claimed that the plumbing company was the one that didn't do its job right and should be held responsible for all the subsequent problems. With this countersuit, there was another round of exchanging information and bills of particulars sent back and forth. This lawsuit now involved four law firms. One was on my side, and three were on the defendants. Even though I wasn't the one to file the suit against them, the plumbing company's lawyers joined the fight against me instead of against the gas company that dragged them into this case.

It was as if all these legal parties had teamed up and were on a mission to prove the gas leaks didn't trigger my disease so they could all walk away scot-free, too. The more time passed, the bigger this case seemed to get, and we still hadn't presented anything to a judge or jury.

Chapter 10: The Frye Test

Once all the legal parties had deposed all the relevant parties, the next phase we needed to get through was the *Frye Test*, also known as a *Frye Hearing*.

This hearing is unique for two reasons. First, it is in front of a judge, and no jury is involved. Second, it considers the evidence either party wants to use in the trial to determine if it is generally accepted by the scientific community. A Frye Test is always done for *novel* scientific information, methods, tests, and research, i.e., anything classified as *experimental*. So, the goal during this trial is not to prove that information or tests are true or reliable. It is just to prove that relevant scientific communities agreed on the evidence.

This particular test arose from a case in 1923, namely *Frye vs. the United States*. In this case, the defendant, convicted of second-degree murder, argued the court should let his expert witness present the results of an experimental lie detector test. However, the medical community had not verified this test as being accurate at the time. The court decided that since the defendant couldn't prove the result of this experimental lie detector was recognized by other scientific authorities, its results would not be accepted. The point of the Frye Test is to stop people from bringing *"junk science"* by so-called expert witnesses in the hopes of winning lawsuits without any scientific basis.

There are three ways scientific evidence can pass a Frye Test:

1. Provide expert testimony that shows there is a general acceptance in the relevant scientific community
2. Provide authoritative scientific writings like reports that show the information is generally accepted by the relevant scientific community.

3. The court uses Frye Test verdicts from other cases to show general acceptance in the relevant scientific community.

You will notice in all of the conditions mentioned above, there is the phrase *relevant scientific community*, which leads to a very important question. Who falls under *relevant*? Medical research falls under multiple scientific disciplines, with many fields branching into others.

Just look at my case with Huntington's. Many specialists, such as geneticists, neurologists, psychologists, radiologists, epidemiologists, and toxicologists, study this disease. And those are just a few names because that is just the nature of research nowadays. There is so much overlap across disciplines.

Secondly, how do you prove *general acceptance*? The Frye Test doesn't have any specific number. All it says is *widespread but not universal*. Do I need 10 doctors to support my claim or 100?

This was one of the most complex aspects of my claim because the right doctors and scientists had to agree with what was going on with me. In other words, I needed to prove that most doctors accepted the theory that Huntington's disease can be triggered by external factors such as exposure to toxic gas. This was a monumental challenge. By this point in my life, I had lost faith in the *general medical community*. For God's sake, the doctors in New York had me running in circles because they couldn't diagnose my condition!

Half of the *relevant medical community* was behind in their medical knowledge in the first place. Let's not forget that many of them said it was impossible for me to even have Huntington's in the first place. This is a statement I still find so bizarre as I sit here all these years later with 39 CAG repeats – a positive diagnosis.

Even though the state of New York still uses Frye Tests, it has garnered much criticism over the years. Firstly, it has become increasingly difficult to label who falls under *relevant*, with so much information falling under multiple fields.

Additionally, the Frye Test fails to recognize the latest scientifically proven evidence or complex scientific testimony because enough people haven't heard about it. This conservative approach means a great deal of accurate information gets ignored. To top it all off, when it comes to Frye, lower courts don't apply this test equally because they do not fully understand the scope. So, there is no standard for assessing expert testimony or scientific information, which allows uncertainty in a case.

Maybe a different court or different judge will allow the testimony. Who can say for sure? There is just so much uncertainty in our legal system. Not to mention, there are so many people trying to take advantage of this uncertainty to win some money that those with real problems have to suffer the consequences. Sure, all these legal tests are necessary to filter out fake claims, but what about people dealing with the impossible that has never been seen or heard before? There is always a patient zero. How do we get a fair trial?

***

As my lawsuit progressed, I learned about all these "*toxic torts road bumps,*" and each revelation made the whole thing more daunting. Even my lawyer told me my case was a tough one because it was one of a kind, but I wasn't going to give up.

However, when my lawyer discovered that Columbia Presbyterian Hospital partly sponsored the Venezuela Project, I will say that it gave me a shred of hope. Even though this hospital did not give me a Huntington's test back then, it was funding research into environmental factors that increase the risks of developing HD in non-white people.

So that meant some legitimate research was out there, which was a promising start. Since I was the one who had filed this lawsuit on the claim that the natural gas and carbon monoxide exposure had triggered my Huntington's disease to start before its time, it was my team's job to prove this *novel theory*. My legal team put together an expert panel of witnesses that included the following people:

- Dr. L, my treating physician and neurologist
- Dr. P, a toxicologist
- Mr. T, an architectural and structural engineer

To counter my claim and essentially poke holes in my early onset case were the experts from the defense's side, namely:

- Dr. M, a neurologist
- Dr. R, a toxicologist

Each of these experts was asked a series of questions that ranged from their experience dealing with HD patients and my condition to what they understood about gas exposure and its toxicity. Both sides, i.e., the plaintiff and defendant's lawyers, examined and cross-examined the experts. This was an extremely rigorous process. Every statement made by an expert was examined word for word, with each side looking for the tiniest of assumptions to tear apart the expert's testimony.

Chapter 11: Expert Testimony

With all this evidence and research in hand, it was now the task of the experts on our side to prove that gas exposure led to hypoxia, which put in oxidative stress, damaging my body at a cellular level and triggering the early onset of my HD symptoms. When my doctor, Dr. L, started giving his testimony, he began by laying out his credentials and clinical expertise, followed by his interactions with me when I first met with him in January 2012.

He explained the symptoms I exhibited, such as chorea, and how he immediately recognized it as a sign he had seen in HD patients. My distinct symptoms were the reason he determined a genetic test was necessary. He also ran other diagnostic tests to confirm the HD diagnosis and check for other underlying problems. My results confirmed his suspicions as they revealed:

- A genetic test that showed 39 CAG repeats
- An MRI revealing white matter disease and basal ganglia damage
- A neuro-conductor velocities (NCV) test that revealed neuropathy in my legs

Dr. L explained how the results from the MRI and NCV tests were consistent with the existence of a toxin in my body and not because of HD. According to his research, many studies have shown that toxin exposure can lead to the kind of nerve damage I had. He also stated that just because the gas company got involved in July 2011 didn't mean the gas leaks began then.

In fact, Dr. L believed I could have been exposed to these harmful gases for much longer, possibly since I had first moved into the apartment.

And since the carbon monoxide detector had gone off in my apartment and I had multiple blood tests and CAT scans showing foreign toxins in my body, he concluded I was living in an environment where the oxygen levels were below optimum.

Remember, during this time, doctors were dismissing me left and right, and none of them wanted to do any further investigation. So, I didn't have lab reports from those days, and my experts couldn't specify an exact timeline of exposure and blood concentrations. Dr. L tried his best to use all the clinical research he collected to show living in an oxygen-deprived environment for a prolonged period puts the body in a medical state known as hypoxia, which leads to oxidative stress. This serious condition damages the body in many ways and has multiple consequences, such as exacerbating underlying conditions.

Dr. T, our toxicologist, agreed with Dr. L's conclusions on oxidative stress as he had extensively studied the effects of toxins on the body. He explained to the court this state causes chemical instability that ultimately causes damage to vital parts of the brain. Both these medical experts explained that even though no clinical studies specifically examine the relationship between natural gas, carbon monoxide, and HD cases, it didn't mean gas exposure could not trigger my HD symptoms, especially considering plenty of evidence showing some relation.

Also, they kept stressing that my diagnosis was *reduced penetrance* and how, in all recorded cases, symptoms manifested later in life, if at all, and with much less severity than the ones I was experiencing.

Given my rare case and the lack of understanding among the doctors, Dr. L believed that more investigation was necessary before any connection between HD and toxic gas exposure could be dismissed completely. Dr. T also agreed with this statement and added it is possible for toxic gas to trigger an asymptomatic case of Huntington's disease before its time. Dr. L also explained how he reasoned my case with a differential diagnosis, a practice regularly used by healthcare providers to understand the nature and cause of a patient's condition. There are three steps to this.

- **Step one** is making a diagnosis based on the symptoms the patient is suffering
- **Step two** is determining whether or not the exposure to natural gas, methane, and carbon monoxide causes enough harm to injure me
- **Step three** is evaluating other potential causes that could explain my symptoms

Combining his years of experience and expertise, with the research he had gathered, Dr. L's differential diagnosis was:

1. Huntington's disease is caused by the degeneration of *striatal neurons*, specific cells found in the central nervous system

2. The faulty HD gene damaged these cells by disrupting the generation of mitochondria.

3. I had none of the other potential risk factors known for Huntington's disease, including:
   o A family history of HD
   o A history of substance abuse
   o Overuse of pharmaceuticals

     ○ Other toxic exposure within my apartment or from any other environment, such as a workplace

4. Prolonged exposure to natural gas and carbon monoxide led to hypoxia and put my body under oxidative stress.

5. Prolonged oxidative stress resulted in more cell and DNA damage.

6. DNA damage also affected the faulty HD gene in my body, which made it unstable and triggered it to become active

7. The activation of the HD gene in my body resulted in the earlier onset of HD symptoms.

Dr. L clearly mentioned that there was no alternative explanation for the early onset of my symptoms. He told the court that medical literature and studies have clearly established that even though reduced penetrance patients like myself are at risk of developing HD, they most likely will not. If they do, it is later in life.

Moving on to the architectural engineer on our panel, Mr. T, who had actively managed gas leak situations since graduating from college. Mr. T had years of experience dealing with natural gas leaks and understood the dynamics of it. He also confirmed that I was dealing with continuous gas exposure and agreed I had been exposed for a prolonged period based on the following evidence:

1. I smelled gas in 2010, as did a gas company employee
2. Two pipes in my apartment building failed integrity tests
3. The gas company agreed that a new meter was needed

4. The gas company had to shut down its gas service to my apartment in July 2011.

He also established that I lived in conditions that did not have any natural or mechanical ventilation, saying that this led to oxygen displacement. He calculated that the gas exposure in my apartment was between 2.7 – 3% most times, and my kitchen window would have to open for more than 20 hours daily to dissipate all the leaking gas.

However, he could not say for sure exactly how many hours I lived in such conditions. None of the experts on my team could, and neither could I really. When dealing with bizarre, unexplainable medical issues, the last thing you think about is how often you open and close your kitchen window. I only knew I spent most of my time in my apartment sick. Given the information available, such as the size of the leak in the pipe, Mr. T calculated the amount of gas he believed would have been present in my apartment. Still, it was only an estimation because the gas company did not give us the gas meter reading from that period.

You will notice that none of our experts could say anything with 100% conviction because my case was just that unique. With no one else in the world like me, there was no comparable data, no clinical studies. Everything was based on extrapolating information that was already available from data that was based on different cases.

Unfortunately, the defense focused heavily on this lack of direct evidence during their cross-examination. First, with our doctors, Dr. L and Dr. T, the defense highlighted their lack of interaction with HD patients. For Dr. L, this is completely untrue. Even though I was the only Huntington's patient Dr. L was treating at the time, he had over two decades of experience treating patients like me.

It was highly unethical to disregard his years of clinical practice and only consider current cases. And while Dr. T did not treat HD patients directly, he was well acquainted with their pathology. Both these doctors are experts in their fields, and their information should remain valid.

Second, they kept asking Dr. L and Dr. P if any *scientific literature submitted* used natural gas or carbon monoxide as the neurotoxic being tested. Unfortunately, none of them did. The defense knew this but wanted both doctors to say it on the record so it sounded like toxic gases had no effects on HD patients.

The defense's medical doctor, Dr. M was adamant that he had never seen an article that showed a link between natural gas and HD. He also stated that throughout his career, he had never seen any scientific study that supported the idea that carbon monoxide or natural gas could:

- Cause Huntington's Disease
- Modify the genetic mutation that causes Huntington's Disease
- Trigger the onset of Huntington's Disease
- accelerate the course of Huntington's Disease

He also said that my team did not provide any *review article* that looks back at all the evidence we presented and concluded something along the lines of, "*We now believe this factor is important to the age of onset because there are these lab studies, animal's studies, or human studies.*"

The defense also dismissed the Venezuela Project, saying it does not mention natural gas or CO exposure, so it was inaccurate and not worth considering.

In all of their grandstanding, they failed to acknowledge *why* there were no studies into the effects of this gas. Researchers never thought to study a possible connection between there wasn't a case. There was no patient zero, but that doesn't mean it is invalid.

Furthermore, the defense was obsessed with this statistic: *2% of people with reduced-penetrance HD are likely to develop the condition naturally.* They kept asking our doctors if they agreed to this information, trying to trap them into admitting I would get Huntington's no matter what. It didn't help that Dr. M kept generalizing his *expert* opinions and using statistics about full penetrance HD. He said I fell in the right age range when I first showed symptoms, between 31 – 89 years old. Can you believe this range? It spans 58 years!

Not once did this doctor even consider that none of the patients with the same onset age as me had symptoms as severe as mine. Of course, the defense didn't care to associate anything with my specific condition. To them, it was simple. I had the CAG repeats, so I had Huntington's. Another point the defense focused on was the lack of records of my early symptoms. They were adamant that any number of illnesses could have caused the earlier problems, even though I was never sick during that time.

Along with this, the defense also claimed that maybe I was showing signs of Huntington's before moving into the apartment and kept asking our expert doctors if that was possible. Of course, the problem here was neither of our doctors could deny it. Everything is possible when you don't have the evidence to say otherwise. Dr. M really built up this line of defense, saying many illnesses and even breathing problems, like asthma, could have put my body under oxidative stress.

How this doctor could equate over a year of toxic gas exposure to non-threatening conditions is beyond my understanding. The two are in no way similar. I was continuously exposed to the gas, with very few breaks for my body to recover.

To make matters worse, the defense wanted Dr. L to give definite answers to their impossible questions, such as:

- *What reduced oxygen levels are required to trigger the expression of HD in a person with reduced penetrance HD?*

- *What levels of natural gas would be needed to cause someone with 39 repeat units to manifest the disease?*

- *What level of hypoxia or the length of time is necessary to cause someone with 39 repeat units to manifest the disease?*

Unfortunately, he could not answer these questions and said exactly that.

Apart from my health, the defense also claimed that because the carbon monoxide alarm only rang once while living in the apartment, it was more likely a false alarm or a faulty device. So, according to them, I was never exposed to any CO.

It is so frustrating to have all the symptoms that point to CO poisoning but not have any proof to back it up. One official meter reading or medical record from those early days would have saved me so much trouble. But it never occurred to me to check the CO levels in my home when the alarm first went off or tell the ER staff to check my blood. Dr. M reviewed my medical records and pointed out that they indicated involuntary movements in my feet and fingers as early as March and April 2010. According to him, I showed symptoms of HD before the gas confirmed the gas leak.

This doctor's logic baffles me. Just because my gas problems weren't being investigated until 2011, it doesn't mean that is when they started, so how could he say otherwise so confidently?

Remember how I mentioned I smelt something weird when I walked into my apartment in 2009? I knew something was wrong, but I believed the landlord and was too naïve to investigate. And so the defense ran with this alternate reality and questioned our experts if it was possible for me to have HD in those days. Our doctors could not deny it because, as I said before, there is always a possibility. Without any medical records, it is difficult to say.

The defense also asked the court to disregard the testimony of Mr. T, our engineer, saying that his analysis and calculations failed to prove anything. Remember, Mr. T only had a limited amount of information to work with, so he could only estimate how much gas was in my apartment at any time. When cross-examined, Mr. T admitted to making the following assumptions in his calculations:

- Using a thicker gas pipe diameter than the one that was in my apartment

- Disregarding any indirect ventilation, such as fresh air, that can pass through the cracks around the walls and windows.

- Assuming a constant gas level in my apartment

- Assuming I was not opening the doors or windows of my apartment

- Assuming the gas level never fluctuated

The defense quickly tore these assumptions to shreds, countering each calculation point. They accused Mr. T of overestimating the amount of gas I was exposed to. Also, they argued that just because the gas reading near the stove was 3%, it didn't mean that it was the amount of gas in the whole apartment.

And while Mr. T admitted that is true, he also pointed out that gas poisoning is still highly possible even if there are different levels in an apartment. But the defense was interested in entertaining possibilities. Their world was black and white, with no shades of gray. I was either exposed to a lethal amount of gas or not. And according to their conservative calculations, I never was in any danger. Unfortunately, my team had no official readings or documentation to prove them wrong.

But the defense was not done twisting the facts. They also told the court that my body could not have been under oxidative stress at any time. According to their experts, the oxygen level needed to go below 17% to be harmful. So even if there was a gas leak of 3% in my apartment, the oxygen level would only go as far down as 20.3%, which was perfectly safe. The defense conveniently omitted the fact that my body was fighting for its life, dealing with system-wide inflammation that stopped my lungs from functioning at full capacity. So, even the slightest dip of oxygen in my apartment was enough to put my body in oxidative stress.

However, the defense was not interested in my specific medical conditions or circumstances. They just threw every health-related generalization available to make it sound like my deteriorating health was nothing more than a medical fluke with no scientific precedence. Remember, this was the Frye Test, and right now, it was all about the science. Even though the negligence and ignorance of the gas company were obvious, it was not under the spotlight.

So, I waited patiently for the court's final decision, praying with my heart and soul that justice would prevail and the system would acknowledge the accuracy of our testimony. I wholeheartedly believed that our panel of experts presented the stronger case, with much more researched information related directly to my condition and justified my claims.

I believed the court was not blind. They would recognize the conditions I was living in and the symptoms it triggered. There was too much evidence to ignore, and I had to believe that would be enough to help me push my lawsuit forward.

Chapter 12: The Court's Decision

As I waited for the court to review all the expert testimony presented for my case and give its decision, the world became unrecognizable. This period was the time of the COVID-19 pandemic when the world was brought to a complete standstill.

I was studying for my bachelor's in Manhattan during this fateful year, and it was one of the cities hardest hit. With the extensive social distancing mandates and repeated lockdowns, living in the city became extremely challenging. I felt more isolated than ever. As much as I tried to make do with my situation, I had reached my limit. I knew my time in New York was over. I had been on my own for too long, and in the middle of the pandemic, I realized I did not want to live like this anymore. So, I made the decision to return home to Cleveland and wait for the court's decision there.

On February 14th, 2021, I officially returned to my hometown and continued my treatment with the Cleveland Clinic. Life here was drastically different than in New York in every way. Most importantly, I was supported by doctors, family and friends. I could literally feel a safety net around me, holding me together.

Thank God for it because, on April 5th, 2022, just two months after I moved back to Cleveland, the court finally gave its verdict regarding the Frye Test, as quoted below:

"The plaintiff failed to meet her burden in showing specific causation... Complaints and cross claims against [the defendant] dismissed... Nothing in the record indicates that [the defendant's] conduct contributed to or exacerbated the plaintiff's condition."

The court said I had not supplied enough evidence to prove the gas exposure had triggered my Huntington's disease. In other words, the defendants were not in the wrong. My expert testimony had failed the Frye Test. So, in the end, my decade-long legal battle would never see the inside of a courtroom or be presented in front of a jury.

Devastation does not even begin to cover the myriad of emotions I went through immediately after receiving this verdict. At first, I was in shock and disbelief that despite all the evidence… despite all the research… the court somehow sided with the side that essentially attacked my very existence. This feeling quickly made way for deep betrayal and an agonizing pain with the realization that the legal system I so firmly trusted and supported as a paralegal had turned its back on me. Then, the anger and despair burst forth, sending me spiraling down a dark abyss of hopelessness.

I had lost my case. That was the only thought in mind for weeks. As much as it hurt to first learn about my Huntington's diagnosis, this felt even worse. It was like a blow to the gut that absolutely eviscerated you from the inside out. Within a three-page document, the State of New York completely invalidated all the suffering I had experienced in the last ten years, summarizing it as, *"Yes, you may feel wronged, but your health issues were inevitable."*

And you know what the worst part of all this is? My case didn't even get the chance to point out the neglect of the gas company! This company and my former landlords got away scot-free even though I had the evidence to prove how they wronged me. Following the court's decision, I questioned every aspect of my experience, from the aptitude of the medical professionals around me to the capabilities of our legal system. I even started questioning the court's decision in light of my skin color.

In the presence of so much damning evidence, my mind could not help but connect it to my race, and so I found myself asking, what would have been the verdict if I was not a person of color? What if I was a white woman? Would the testimony from my experts still have failed the Frye Test? These questions festered in my mind for a long time because the truth is that no matter how similar situations and circumstances are, race is a factor, and justice is not equal for all. It is disproportionate against people of color.

As a paralegal, I know my rights as a citizen of the US. I thought this would make me better prepared to handle the legalities and navigate the system. Yet my know-how was no match for the deep-rooted racial parasite living in our legal system. My voice was silenced, and so I did not get justice.

My experience solidified the belief that people of color are not considered equal to white people. Hence, they will always be treated differently. I have always seen the signs and even witnessed the change in body language and tone when I walk into certain spaces, but in my heart, I always hoped that things would change. I remember when Barack Obama was voted the first black president of our country. It was an exciting day for us all, like we had taken a giant leap forward. And yet, it was nothing more than a fleeting moment.

I see now that even though we are collectively more educated as a nation, have access to incredible technology, and are standing up for our rights as individuals, our legal system is still stuck in the past. It still perceives and considers ethnicity heavily, allowing it to influence verdicts. This unfairness is mind-boggling.

I am certain that from the moment I filed my case as an African American, I was demoted as a person and deemed unworthy of justice. It makes me think back to the era when doctors used to do experiments on black women because we were akin to guinea pigs who could be experimented on.

My words probably feel bleak, but this is the harsh reality. People of color do not get the justice they deserve. They get harsher punishments, are jailed on insufficient evidence, and are not trusted as much as white plaintiffs in toxic tort cases. If you take the time to examine other legal cases, you will see a clear distinction in how white plaintiffs are processed and judged.

Given this tough racial obstacle, we must be louder and more persistent. We have to fight for our rights. The more noise we make collectively, the more we will be heard, which is the only way to break the system. So, my advice to black women or any woman of color who feels they have been legally wronged is to demand justice. Trust your intuition, be it a toxic tort issue like mine or any other personal injury situation like a car accident. Contact lawyers and study to know your rights and where you stand legally. If we do not stand up for ourselves, the system will not.

If you are up against a company like I was, you must be all the more prepared. Save all documentation. Take photos and make videos. Record all interactions. Companies, especially multimillion-dollar ones, will not come forward to own up to their mistakes. And never in a million years will they step forward to rectify any wrongdoing. Unfortunately, the dominant business strategy many of these companies follow is to sweep mistakes under the carpet and shred the evidence. So be ready to smash through walls because that is what it will feel like going against them.

Ultimately, in-depth due diligence is key. The more research you do and the more you find out about your case and its causation, the stronger your case will be so you can get the justice that is rightfully yours.

Also, be prepared to fight harder and longer. You will find yourself against a centuries-old bias that will make every second an uphill battle. You will be judged against different criteria that will put everything from your character to your personal choices under the microscope. It will be unfair and hurtful, but you must stand proud and demand to be seen and heard. Hopefully, following this advice, you will get a fair verdict and what you deserve. However, I will reiterate that no matter how thorough you are, justice may not prevail. Just look at me. I did the work and had the evidence, but the court said it was not enough.

Honestly, after all those years of fighting in court, it took a lot of time to process that unjust verdict. I will admit that one of the reasons it was so difficult was because I was too naïve. Before the court's decision, I had not considered my testimony could fail the Frye Test. In my head, losing was never a possibility because I was so sure my case was airtight.

But this confidence meant I was completely unprepared when the court said I had not proved the gas exposure specifically triggered my Huntington's disease. I was so angry to hear this that I had a very hard time letting it go. There was a dark cloud over me, and it just intensified my hatred for the people who had wronged me.

It took time, but I finally came to the realization that this negative feeling, although justified, was essentially a poison eating my mind and soul. It was locking me in a state of anger that was stopping me from moving forward. And here is another instance where God's plan for me was apparent. Had I received this verdict in New York, I don't know what I would have done. I don't know if I would still be here to share my story. He moved me out of that toxic environment, just two months before the verdict, to a place of healing in Cleveland.

Here, I was surrounded by an incredible support system of family, friends, and doctors. They gave me the space to vent my frustration, the therapy to process, and ultimately, the strength to accept my situation.

Even though I am a spiritual person, my anger had completely clouded my vision, so I couldn't see beyond my case and take in the bigger picture. It was only through regular therapy and counseling, that I was finally able to lift my lead head out of that fog and see a life outside of this legal battle.

I now see that against all odds, my life was spared. I was exposed to toxic gases, but I lived totally avoiding the deadly consequences. Therefore, the time I have now is a gift, and I am not going to waste any more of it being angry. I learned that I deserved more, and I deserved better. So, I made the conscious decision to lead my best life going forward to transform the sad events of my past into a positive story filled with triumphs and achievements.

At the end of the day, I accept that I am not in control. I am not the Authority, so I don't have the power to change my destiny. It will follow its own path, and those who have done wrong will reap what they have sown. Karma does not see race, ethnicity, religion, or bank statements. It is the true justice that treats everyone equally, so if you are guilty of something, you will get yours in the end.

I take great solace in this fact, and it has served greatly in helping me get through my darker days. Even as I sit here and look back at everything that has happened, I feel flashes of anger rising up. Still, they settle much more quickly because, like I said, I am 100% focused on living my best life.

As a 48-year-old woman with Huntington's disease, I have unabashedly put my health first over everything else, even my emotions.

 I don't have the time or space for any form of negativity because I need to keep my stress levels as low as possible, as it helps manage my symptoms so I can keep living with this neurodegenerative disease.

Chapter 13: Healing in Cleveland

Moving to Cleveland has proven to be the best decision I have made for my health and emotional well-being in a long time. And it was not only because I was back in my hometown. This city is home to the Cleveland Clinic, a world-renowned institution at the forefront of innovative medical research and clinical trials for numerous conditions.

Within this center, there is an entire department dedicated to Huntington's disease that was established in partnership with the HDSA. It has some of the best doctors and healthcare providers in the world from a variety of different medical fields, working together to monitor and treat patients like me with Huntington's disease. Not only do they look at Huntington's disease holistically, but they also have some of the most effective medicines and therapies currently available and even under research.

Even though I had excellent care in New York with Dr. L, the level of professionalism at the Cleveland Clinic was beyond my expectations. There were no questions, no doubts, or suspicions. Here, the doctors didn't say nonsensical things like *"Black people can't get Huntington's."*

All I had to do was show them my genetic test results, and almost immediately, a team of doctors was assembled. They began running diagnostic tests and developing treatment plans. No one assumed I was on drugs or an alcoholic. Each question was focused on understanding the most about my medical history, current health, and presenting symptoms. I finally received the respect I craved back in New York.

Given their close association with the HDSA, the doctors at the Cleveland Clinic knew more about Huntington's disease than anywhere else.

They were much more open-minded to this illness's multifaceted nature, understanding that factors other than genetics were at play. The doctors were very curious about my story and wanted to know everything about my family history and experiences. Each one was just as appalled as the next to learn how I was treated by the NYC doctors and how difficult it was for me to get the genetic test for HD. They were especially shocked by how many doctors ignored the classic symptoms of Huntington's disease just because I was African American.

As I explained more about my situation and the gas exposure issue, many doctors at the Cleveland Clinic agreed to the possibility of the toxic gas triggering my condition! I cannot begin to tell you how important that was for me to hear. During the legal battle, the defense's heartless attempts to dehumanize my condition wounded me mentally and emotionally. So, to hear well-versed medical professionals agree with me and say, *"Yes, this is possible,"* was especially validating and healing.

Another exciting aspect of being a patient at this medical institute is that I am also part of a significant Huntington's disease community, there to support one another in numerous ways. So, even though Huntington's disease has limited my ability to work in public service on a larger scale, it has not stopped me completely. I can still find ways to be helpful and supportive to other patients, even on my bad days, which is still very rewarding.

As much as I love Manhattan, that city has given me a great deal of traumatic stress. There are so many ill feelings housed on that small island that I don't think I can ever go back. I don't know what the future holds for me, but for now, Cleveland is where I am most comfortable.

Also, this city makes sense because it was my home for a long time. This is where I grew up and where all my best memories are. So it is no wonder I have found more peace of mind here as well as space!

I have upgraded from that teeny tiny apartment in Midtown to a much more spacious duplex. Now, I have a separate kitchen, living room and dining room. After living in New York for so long, cramped with all my stuff, I forgot just how nice it is to have actual physical space around me. For once, I can literally breathe again.

Despite the added amenities, I will say that life back home hasn't been the easiest. Even though I have access to better doctors and treatment, stress and anxiety are ever present, always looming right over my head. Nowadays, the issue that weighs heaviest on my mind is my mother and her health. My mother has also been diagnosed with Huntington's disease and is presenting with many symptoms. On top of this, she also suffered a stroke not long after I moved back.

While the stroke was not because of Huntington's, it temporarily blocked the blood supply to my mother's brain, which is known to cause brain damage. This, in turn, can lead to numerous cognitive and physical disabilities. Not only is my mother managing the effects of her neurodegenerative condition, but she is also dealing with the complications following the stroke. As much as I try to take care of her, I am painfully aware of how much help I need to take care of myself. So there is only so much I can do.

Often, the most I have to offer is my presence, so I try to spend as much time with her as possible so she does not feel alone. Also, as time has passed, I have become an advocate for my mother's health.

Even though my father is legally her health proxy, he is often overwhelmed by all the medical decisions that need to be made. Given what I know and what I have learned dealing with doctors over the years, I try my best to help my dad make the best treatment choices for my mom.

While I am happy to be more involved in my mother's life, witnessing every moment has been difficult. As the days and weeks go by, I see her succumb to ever-worsening symptoms as the disease progresses, among which the paranoia is particularly extreme.

Paranoia is a common symptom of Huntington's disease, but just because it happens to most HD patients doesn't make it any easier to see. It is painful watching my mother live in constant anxiety, believing everyone around her, even loved ones, is out to harm her.

It is hard to witness these ongoing changes firsthand, especially knowing there is nothing I can do to reverse the effects. My mother now feels like a completely different person. Even if she doesn't always remember things about herself, I sometimes catch a glimpse of my mother's true personality from time to time. But those moments are fleeting and becoming fewer and fewer.

I have so much love and sympathy for my mother as she continues to live in this fearful state, but I can't help but feel very scared for myself. I can't help but look at her and wonder if this will be me in 20 years. I know the stroke also has its hands in her symptoms, and not everything she is going through is because of Huntington's. Still, there is no way of knowing for sure.

Hence, I cannot help but think more about what will happen to me down the road. It is hard and painful to think about a future filled with medical problems, but I can't ignore the truth of my situation. At the end of the day, we can't hide from our problems.

That is why I believe that when it comes to your health, ignorance is *not* bliss. The best thing you can do for yourself is to be direct and honest. If you feel like something is wrong with your body, then something is wrong with your body. Trust your intuition and see a doctor. You know your body better than anyone else, and no one can tell you that something is not wrong. If a doctor is shutting you out, don't waste your time. Find a new one. Research your area and find specialists who will take you seriously and study your health anomaly. At the same time, be bold and ask questions as they examine you. This is not the time to be shy. Demand doctors justify their diagnosis and get the tests you need.

Honestly, this advice is for any person because health issues can happen to anyone. But for African American women, this approach and attitude is especially important. Again, look at me. Since Huntington's disease is not seen in black people, I struggled and suffered more than necessary to become diagnosed.

Having said that, I was diagnosed over a decade ago, and since then, the medical field has made significant strides. In that regard, it is slightly easier for people to get more objective care. However, there is still room for improvement, especially concerning the interconnection of diseases, gender, and race. Ethnicities are so mixed in this age that we cannot box any disease or medical condition to a specific race.

I am sure that if we re-examined our families' medical histories, we would find many instances where classic symptoms were ignored or mislabeled under the wrong disease. In my case, maybe my grandmother or great-grandfather had Huntington's, but I have no way of knowing.

So, relying on family history or looking for a condition in a family tree is not enough. We need to broaden our medical understanding to such a degree and normalize that anyone, regardless of ethnicity, is susceptible to any illness.

As I said earlier, the medical world has made strides, but there are still doctors following ancient theories. As patients, we need to be more vocal, magnifying this bias and advocating for ourselves so we get the treatment we deserve.

However, do not make the mistake of using Google for every symptom. The internet is not a doctor and just gives you the most serious conditions from the most popular websites. Honestly, it will drive you nuts and panic for no reason, so seek professional medical advice. The sooner you know what is affecting your body, the better you can take care of yourself. Even more important, if you find out you have a disease or condition, reach out for help so you can find your support as quickly as possible.

When I moved back to Cleveland, I found a medical community to support me, and I am more grateful for them with every passing day. Part of this community is my specialized doctors, who are experts in their field and my disease. These professionals give me all the medical support I need to manage my symptoms. They make me feel like I am part of the team, and together, we develop a plan that will help me the most. All I have to do is follow the steps.

Of course, medication is a big part of that. I have to take a cocktail of various potent drugs to control and mask many of my symptoms. One of the most effective is Xenazine, and it has been a lifesaver. This drug masked those awful involuntary body movements so well that I am no longer shaking excessively. If I still had to deal with that symptom, I would have been a wreck, depressed, and perhaps even suicidal.

But even starting a new treatment plan was a journey because of the many side effects of these new medicines. Thankfully, my doctors kept me well-informed, so I was never taken by surprise and had an idea about how my body would react. One of the most common side effects I experienced was fatigue. After my dose, I would be so tired and lethargic that I'd fall asleep for a couple of hours. Luckily, my body has slowly adjusted over time, so the effects are not as strong as they used to be. Now and then, I do still feel tired, but not enough to put me to sleep.

The other vital part of my medical community is my tribe – a group of Huntington's patients who I meet with regularly once a month. These special people give me the emotional support and strength to keep going. We discuss our lives and how things are progressing every time we connect. And let me tell you, there is nothing more comforting than talking to others like me who are going through the same illness and managing the same symptoms. It combats all the feelings of isolation that tormented me in New York, and I feel seen and heard. Interestingly, listening to their stories and journeys has also humbled me in many ways.

I think about how many of them have known Huntington's disease has been a part of their families for many years and have had to bury countless relatives because of it. As I mentioned earlier, Huntington's disease is an autosomal dominant illness, so all it takes is one faulty HD gene from one parent. That means if either of your parents has the gene, you have a 50/50 chance of developing the disease.

These are terrifying odds. So, to hear how some patients have had to grow up watching loved ones succumb to Huntington's and know that maybe the same thing would happen to them was shocking. I can't even imagine what life as a child in such a household would be like.

As someone who was diagnosed as an adult after living a carefree childhood, it breaks my heart. When you are young, the world is supposed to be filled with big dreams and possibilities. But these kids grew up with a dark future in front of their eyes where they knew one day they would end up with the same illness that took their loved ones.

Yet, as I talked to them and they shared stories of the good days and the bad, I learned more about how they have continued to make the most of their lives to find joy. We all know that one day, we will lose control of our bodies, but every member of my tribe makes an effort to delay it for as long as possible. I am inspired by everyone's bravery and zeal for life.

It encourages me to do the same and push myself to lead a fulfilling life. Even on my darkest days, I have this community to lean on, and I consider myself extremely fortunate. I always encourage anyone with a chronic or terminal illness to seek their community and connect with their tribe.

Linking with specialists and other patients is so important because it is not just about finding a treatment and exchanging information. It is also about finding the physical, mental, and emotional support to keep going.

As for affording the treatment itself, I know how expensive it can be, so it is best to explore your options. If you have insurance, check what your plan includes. Insurance coverage varies from provider to provider and depends on several factors. However, in most cases, it should cover some aspect of treatment, such as medicine or doctor visits. Take some time to dig into your insurance policy details and even talk to the insurance company's customer service to learn absolutely everything so you can pursue the best possible treatment.

Even if you don't have the coverage or are not in the financial position to seek specialized help, you can still reach out to social workers and disease advocacy organizations. Here, you can get the access you need to resources that can help. For example, if you have Huntington's disease, contact the HDSA, or if you have Parkinson's, you can contact the Parkinson's Foundation. With a chronic or debilitating illness, you can also apply for a disability such as Medicare benefits or Medicaid to help cover treatment costs.

Unfortunately, many of the medicines necessary to manage neurodegenerative diseases cost thousands of dollars, making it practically impossible to afford if you are not covered by some form of insurance. So you have to reach out and find help. For all you know, you may be eligible for grants or clinical research that gets you the medical support you need. Still, you won't know until you explore, and the first step is to ask for help.

Chapter 14: Making Peace with My Future

The last decade of my life feels like a never-ending roller coaster of a million miles, as if I have traveled to the moon and back. From the moment I was diagnosed with a terminal illness to where I am now, *so* much has happened, and it has had such a profound effect on me. And I don't just mean in terms of my physical health. I am not the same person. I have grown emotionally and spiritually. With this growth, I have gained a new perspective on life and what it means to me.

In retropspect, I see clearly nothing in my past that could have prepared me for what would happen. Neither of my parents or grandparents had any medical problems, even resembling Huntington's. Hence, this illness was never a part of the conversation. I didn't even know what it was.

And even though I had heard many stories about other people hit by adversity, these stories felt distant. It never occurred to me that I would be in the same boat one day. Growing up, I thought life would be smooth sailing. So, naturally, when I first moved to New York, my mind was filled with all the standard dreams, like visions of living in the big city, working in courthouses, and maybe even starting a family.

Even when my medical problems first started, I didn't fully grasp the gravity of the situation. For one, I was so overwhelmed with doctors, medical tests, and legal proceedings that I never really gave myself the time to think about my future. Honestly speaking, I was far more interested in looking at my past and family history to find answers to all my questions, the most important being *"Why me?"*

Genetically speaking, I have some answers. Given my mother's positive diagnosis, I know Huntington's runs in my maternal family, coming from either my mother's mother or father. My doctors suspect it was probably from my grandmother, but there is no way to be sure. Then, of course, was the fact that I now have a pretty good idea of how the rest of my life will go and, ultimately, end. That happens when you get diagnosed with a terminal illness like Huntington's, and you start looking into the wealth of medical literature now available.

You learn each and every detail of the symptoms you will experience and how you will slowly lose control of yourself. All this information makes it even harder to process the whole diagnosis, so no wonder immediate reactions will be unpleasant. Your emotions will run wild, and you will face an existential crisis, overcome with grief and anger. But these are all valid emotions because your life has changed forever. The second you get a Huntington's diagnosis, you can feel the ground beneath you shift as if you are moving onto a new path.

Personally, I went into a state of mourning. I remember standing at a crossroads not long after my diagnosis, trying to figure out what to make of my life. To me, there were only two ways I could go.

One took me down the path of self-pity, and I would allow it to consume me. Then, all I would feel would be negative emotions such as anger, sadness, and fear. I would stop caring about taking care of myself and just give up. The other was to accept my fate and trust in God's Plan. I would let positive emotions like gratitude and kindness guide me and fight to stay in control for as long as possible.

On paper, it is pretty obvious that the path of acceptance is better. Every self-help book will tell you that. But when you're in the midst of an emotional tornado, nothing is obvious. Acceptance feels like losing, and no one wants to be the loser. For too long, I was stuck in limbo, unable to accept my new life because I could not let go of everything stolen from me, such as my career and family goals.

Honestly, the only way to get out of this and get on the right path is with professional help. It is the only way to break free of the limbo and commit to a better path. I am so grateful I had access to professional therapy and was able to find my community. My support group helped me thoroughly process all my emotions and get through the darkness. This is a vital hurdle to overcome, and it isn't easy. You will be scared and hopeless at times because there's a great deal of unpredictability and uncertainty when it comes to medical illness.

However, you can't let that fear define you. Just because you have an idea of how things might end, you have no idea how each second of your life will go. You must push yourself to think outside of the known and explore the unknown. When you do and come out the other side, you will see life is waiting for you.

Yes, it will be completely different from what you dreamed about, but it doesn't have to be bleak. There will still be hundreds of ways to find happiness, meaning and fulfillment. Think of it this way: now you have more information about your future and can make the most of every minute of it. I take great solace in this.

This is a fantastic quote from Oprah Winfrey that I feel sums up these sentiments quite nicely, *"The greatest discovery of all time is that a person can change his future by merely changing his attitude."* With this outlook, I am solely focused on living my best life in every way possible. I follow a routine, take my medications on time, and eat healthily. I see my doctors regularly and meet my tribe, family, and friends as much as I can. My doctors tell me that stress makes my symptoms worse, so everything I do serves to keep my stress levels down.

I have made the conscious decision to make every effort to live for as long as possible because who knows what the future holds? In 10 – 20 years, there may be better medications that can control the symptoms. There may even be a cure that stops the progression, eventually suspending the degeneration. I want to be around for it.

I am hopeful because neurodegenerative diseases such as Alzheimer's, Huntington's, Parkinson's, and ALS are all within the same wheelhouse. They're all diseases of the basal ganglia, and many of their mechanisms of action overlap. Hence, research in one condition can help promote research in another. So, there is always a chance that things can get better. I choose to stay optimistic and believe that one day, there will be better medications and treatments that help improve the quality of life for everyone. And when I say everyone, I mean everyone.

My experience has given me a new empathy for people and families who have neurological conditions. There is no room in the medical field for racial bias, and every book that says a disease or illness is associated with a specific ethnic group needs to be thrown out. I strive to be the opposite of what I have experienced with biased healthcare providers.

Trust me when I say the best part about my diagnosis is that I now live very much in the present. I have stopped thinking about my past and future because my time now is more valuable than ever. I live with purpose, trying to do the most that I can. I keep myself busy learning new things. After moving back, I kept my promise to myself to hold on to my mind. I enrolled in a community college and began studying graphic design. After a lifetime of being told to concentrate on practical courses, I finally have the chance to explore my creative side. Now, I spend my days reading, researching, writing, and collaborating with others in my program. My health is no longer my only priority.

Also, now that I know everything can change sooner than later, I truly feel like I see more beauty and joy around me. Every day I get is a gift to me, and I cherish every moment.

Having said all this, let me be clear. I'm not living in a world of illusion. I know what is in store for me. I know about my disease and can see my mother, who now lives in a nursing home. So, I am also preparing for that eventuality. For example, I am writing a will and detailed care documents.

By preparing this paperwork now, I make sure the decision-making burden of my treatment does not fall on my relatives. I want my treatment to stay in my control for as long as possible, so even if I cannot give my informed consent, my care documents will tell doctors what to do.

Much of this has been prompted by what is happening with my mother and the fact that she cannot express her desires regarding her medical issues. I have had many discussions with my doctors and contacts at HDSA, exploring different scenarios and the options I will have available. No matter how optimistic I try to be about life, I stay grounded because I cannot deny the inevitable.

I also make it a point to discuss my prognosis with others in my patient groups. Having these conversations and sharing our feelings and frustrations is important because this is all a part of life now. As for my legal battle, I think about it less and less as time goes on. It is possible that there is more information about Huntington's disease nowadays, and perhaps legally, things may be different. But I don't want to go down that path. There is too much stress in fighting a legal case, and that is not good for my health, physically and emotionally.

Dealing with lawyers and courts is not fun for the healthiest person, and I don't want to spend my limited energy on that. What's done is done, and I have found a way to accept it even if it is not fair. The most I can do is raise my voice and make sure as many people as possible hear my story so they don't get stuck where I did. Even if one person learns something from my experience and makes a smarter decision because of my story, I will be happy.

Perhaps the most important thing to come out of my struggle is that now my sister's children are in a better position to get the help they need if they show any symptoms. Now, all they have to do is tell their doctor that their aunt has Huntington's, and they will immediately be tested, no questions asked. They will not have to run around desperately looking for a competent doctor to listen to them like that. And you know what? That gives me great comfort.

At the end of the day, everyone wants their life to have some purpose, to be of some importance – not to be forgotten. No matter what happens to me down the road, I know that my story will help future generations in my family, for better or worse.

Also, my experience can help other women or people of color with similar medical worries. These people may find some guidance or advice as they try to navigate their troubled journeys; in this way, my life feels worth more. It feels more valuable.

Despite everything that has happened to me, and even though I have a neurodegenerative disease that is destroying my body from the inside, my life now serves a bigger purpose. This sense of purpose also helps me make peace with my future. As I mentioned earlier, I am a spiritual person and have come to believe that this was God's Plan, so I have left everything in God's Hands. For anyone else dealing with a terminal illness, this mentality can take a great weight off your shoulders, no matter which higher authority you believe in.

Again, I am not trying to glaze over reality by saying this. Believing in a higher power can be a sanctuary throughout this complicated journey. Holding on to some form of spirituality is like having a hand to hold when you're navigating the darkest corners of your mind and need something to pull you out. In moments when the weight of everything becomes almost unbearable, faith can provide that glimmer of light.

Having faith stops you from asking yourself, *"Why me?"* Instead, it reminds you that there is a reason, even if you don't know what it is. It reminds you that you are not alone in this fight, and a divine presence guides you through it.

When I struggle to understand, my faith becomes a source of hope. It's a belief that there's something greater beyond this life – a realm of peace and healing that awaits. This gives me the strength to face each day and every interaction.

While my faith does not take away all the burden or erase the pain, it shifts how I carry that burden. Somehow, it has infused my life with hope and some peace. My faith is my anchor and my refuge, helping me navigate this challenging journey and easing my heart at the same time.

Chapter 15: Life with Huntington's Disease

It is hard to explain what living with a terminal illness is like because it literally transformed every aspect of everything. It's like a constant companion that has a hand in reshaping my daily routines, how I plan my day, what I want to do, and my relationships with others.

Physically, the changes are undeniable because of the gradual loss of coordination and muscle control. Thankfully, my medications have done a wonderful job of masking many of my symptoms, so on my good days, I find it easier to go about my day. But I have my bad days, too, where the symptoms still peek through, or the side effects of my medicine affect me more than usual. These days are instant reminders of the disease's progression.

I talk to other people with HD regularly, and it's always eye-opening to listen to their daily struggles, compare notes, and give each other advice. Just like I mentioned for myself, everyone has their good days and their bad. On the bad, everyone's challenges usually revolve around simple tasks that most of us take for granted, like walking, dressing, or keeping our balance. Similarly, it gets harder for some to speak and swallow as coordinated muscle movements become compromised with HD.

I think cognitive challenges are the most common for most of us. I deal with forgetfulness and concentration problems. Sudden mood changes are also plenty. I go from feeling happy to sad or anxious in a second for no reason.

Like other HD patients, another struggle is the fluctuating energy level. One day, I am bursting with energy. The next, I feel too lethargic to do anything. On the low days, even the tiniest of decisions seem to take a great deal of effort, and any form of planning is simply out of the question.

I think having Huntington's is like being in a constant battle with your own body. You might want to do something, but your body just won't let you. I really had to re-tune the way I lived my life to adapt to these limitations. Now, I take everything slow, letting my body dictate what I can do. There is no more pushing or forcing myself to do things. I use every tool and aid in the book, asking for help when I need it so it is easier for me to function.

I have also modified how I approach any task. No matter what I need to do, I break it into the smallest, more manageable steps. For example, getting dressed is always a sitting-down task. At the same time, I have simplified my tasks. Making my bed is no longer about creating that picture-perfect layout with all the extra pillows. It's about straightening the sheets and arranging a few pillows.

Also, I have a schedule and reminders for everything, from my medication to my meals. I like to stay ahead of everything for two reasons. One, it removes the unnecessary last-minute stress, and two, I don't forget anything important I need to do.

Despite the challenges, I have found my way to exist. I am happy I can still do all my housework and maintain my house, be it cleaning or doing the laundry. I even prepare meals for myself. I don't know how long I will be able to do all these things by myself, so I relish every moment I can. This may be surprising to hear, but I also keep a gratitude journal. You may be thinking, *"What does a person with Huntington's Disease have to be grateful for?"*

The answer is - a lot! I am grateful for every day I can get out of bed and get on with my day. I am grateful for all the support I have. I am grateful for a million things in my life. Journaling about all the good I have in my life helps me keep a positive attitude and build emotional strength, which keeps me motivated to take care of myself.

With this gratitude, I celebrate all the little victories in my life, giving myself a figurative pat on the back for all my little achievements, no matter how small they may seem to others. What is important is they are huge for me. Maybe it means walking without stumbling or managing to cook an entire meal independently. These moments remind me that I'm strong and capable, even though I'm dealing with challenges. They show that I'm making progress and not giving up. So, when I achieve these small wins, I indulge myself, taking a moment to smile and feel proud of what I did. These victories might not change a thing, but they are one more drop in the pool that helps me stay positive.

When I need to get around the city, like see my doctor or visit my mother, I have access to paratransit. This is a type of transportation specifically for people with a disability. These vehicles are fitted to handle my mobility limitations, and the drivers are trained to assist me if I need help. Even though I can't drive, this service still gives me a sense of independence, making it easier for me to go where I need to without worrying if I am going to have any problems along the way.

As I have adjusted to this new way of life, I am also exploring ways to keep myself mentally stimulated, like taking art classes to learn graphic design. When I started taking these classes, I did not know what to expect if I would be any good at it. But I have quickly come to enjoy these sessions.

Graphic design is like painting on a canvas without the mess. Plus, it also has this element of puzzle solving when you are choosing colors or rearranging elements. But the best part is that there is no right answer. Anything goes! All of this keeps my mind engaged while allowing me to express my creativity.

Also, this desire to keep my brain engaged is how I decide what I want to do. I'm very aware that there are quite a few things I cannot do, given my health, so I have found it is better to focus on what is achievable. Think of it this way: instead of career goals, I have mind-simulation goals. This approach motivated me to complete my bachelor's degree. So, in the same vein, I have a bucket list of all the enrichment classes I want to take. Not only will they keep my mind busy, but they will also give me a place to escape from the stress of my illness and other worries in my life.

Something I did not expect is the strong effect Huntington's has had on my relationships. Some friends and family members have stepped forward with unwavering support and empathy. In contrast, others have struggled to understand the changes I'm going through and have faded away.

I don't hold any ill feelings for those who have stepped away. That is just the nature of human interactions. People come and go. And when it comes to a terminal illness, many of us are emotionally unequipped to deal with those types of feelings. If anything, it just shows me how much an illness like mine can impact the people around me.

Of course, I don't think about the people who are no longer with me. Honestly, I just don't have that kind of time anymore. I am much more occupied connecting with others who are going through similar experiences. I feel much more comfortable with these individuals, knowing I can share my fears, hopes, and triumphs without judgment.

This is also why I would like to attend another Huntington's Disease convention in the near future. It has been a while since I have been able to go as traveling isn't as easy as it used to be.

For me, going to a convention this time around won't be about gathering information. After all, I have access to the best treatment in the world at the Cleveland Clinic. Going this time will give me an opportunity to reconnect with some old friends and meet some new people.

Living with Huntington's disease has really changed every molecule in my body, teaching me what it truly means to live authentically, which is much more than "you do you." It is about being real and honest with yourself, as opposed to fooling yourself to be someone you're not.

When you live authentically, you show your true feelings, thoughts, and desires. You don't hide behind masks or try to fit in just to please others. Instead, you make choices that match who you really are, even if it's not always easy. Living authentically is like embracing your own unique story, with all its ups and downs, and being proud of it.

It's about being confident in your own skin and living a life that feels right for you, even when faced with challenges or uncertainties of a terminal illness, which is constantly reminding you of the fragility of life. It is also for this reason I am my biggest advocate. I have learned to speak up for myself, making sure I am understood and my needs are met. Back in New York, even though I trusted my voice, I always felt like I was scrambling from here to there, reacting to the latest symptom or problem in my life. Not anymore.

Now, I am proactive. I keep myself educated so I can have informed discussions with my healthcare team. I approach my doctors whenever I need to because I feel more empowered. I truly feel more in control of my life than ever before, and it amazes me that it took an illness like Huntington's for me to finally step up.

Maybe this was God's Plan all along: to make a stronger person who will continue to fight and find joy amidst the struggle and leave some lasting impact on the world, no matter the limitations.

Chapter 16: The Journey Continues

As we reach this final chapter, this may be the end of my story for now, but it is very much just the beginning of my journey. As I look ahead, I see a world filled with opportunities, experiences, and moments yet to be cherished. I'm genuinely excited to embrace what the next day and the days beyond, have in store for me.

My dear reader, I want you to share in this optimism and look at your own life the way I look at mine. As a parting gift, here are five ways I keep this hopeful disposition that you can easily adopt in strength yours.

1. Embracing Change and Adapting

One of the most unexpected things I learned on this journey with Huntington's disease was that change is not the enemy. We should neither fear it nor hate it. Change is nothing more than a part of life, like the rising and falling tide.

Imagine the tide swelling up, pushing everything in its path, and then falling back, leaving debris behind as it transforms the shoreline just a little. This is exactly what change does in our life. It flows in, washing away the old and bringing in the new, ultimately reshaping our circumstances. I know this can be scary, and for many of us, the gut instinct is to become defensive and build a figurative wall to try to stop this change from affecting us too much.

I know I used to do that. When I was first diagnosed with Huntington's disease, I tried to hold on to the life I had in New York.

I didn't want my health to change the way I was living, so mentally, I resisted staying longer than I needed to. I refused to accept that this disease was now a major driving force in my life and would dictate a new way of living for me. Then, when my health stopped me from doing anything, I would feel exhausted, depressed, and defeated.

It took me some time to understand that life didn't have to be like this. I did not need to fight these changes because, just like the tide, I could not stop it. Change is inevitable, so why fight it? It was time to embrace this new normal and adapt accordingly.

Truly, the ability to embrace change and grow is a lifeline. Yes, it can be overwhelming, but it makes it much easier to face life's most formidable challenges. Whether that is an unexpected health problem, the end of a long-term relationship, or a sudden career shift, every change can be embraced and used as a catalyst for personal growth.

The day I decided that Huntington's disease was now a part of my life was the moment I flipped the switch, shifting from surviving to thriving. I let go of what I couldn't control and focused on what I could. Did I have to give up certain things? Yes, but in doing so, I discovered a reservoir of inner strength and resilience I never knew I possessed. Instead of dwelling on the limitations and what could have or should have happened, I changed my perspective and found joy in the present.

This is what I want you to do: embrace the changes and challenges in your life. Let them push you out of your comfort zone because you will adapt. You are much stronger than you realize.

2. Learning from Difficult Moments

For many of us, the most challenging moments in our lives come uninvited. These unwelcome guests cast a shadow on our path and have the potential to test us in every way imaginable. They force us to stop and examine ourselves, making us confront our vulnerabilities. This is never an easy task and often comes with pain, which can take a toll on our self-esteem.

However, taking a step back and looking at the bigger picture is important. Firstly, these setbacks are not just signs of weakness or ineptitude. Even though we walk the path of our choosing, there is so much uncertainty and unpredictability on either side that so much is out of our control. Anything can happen. So stop looking at these difficult moments as stumbling obstacles and turn them into stepping stones. While they may cause you to pause, treat them as a teaching moment to look around and re-evaluate your situation instead of just focusing inward.

I have had many difficult times in my life. Still, I have accepted each one because they have given me an encyclopedia of valuable lessons, both practical and profound. I have learned more about renting, real estate, and utility companies than any book could teach me.

I have learned much about the medical field and the healthcare system even without the degree. As I live with this progressive illness, I have learned about the importance of patience, resilience, and compassion. Everything I have learned over the years has made me wiser and more confident in myself.

I encourage you to approach your own challenges with a similar mindset. Don't berate yourself when obstacles fall on your path.

Try to view them as an opportunity to gain some wisdom and a deeper understanding of yourself. The lesson may not always be a massive life-altering realization. In fact, many times, it may be nothing more than, *"I'm never doing that again."* Yet, it is still a lesson that adds a little bit more to your knowledge bank, and that is always worth something.

3. The Power of Community

I have mentioned it before and will say it again because I believe in it so steadfastly: we are social creatures and thrive best in a supportive community. Before Huntington's disease, I thought this *community* referred to the people around me, like my family and friends. But a community is so much more than that.

While it may include your near and dear, it is, in fact, a social network that is there for you, ready to listen when you need to express your feelings, celebrate your highs, and empathize with you during the lows. They are the beacon that gets you through your most challenging storms.

I've witnessed firsthand the profound impact of a supportive network. I am forever grateful to mine, from the doctors and therapists who treat me to the other patients in my support group. Each one of these individuals is another frame in the scaffolding that holds me together.

In the search for this community, you may find you have to leave certain people behind. I know I had to. This can be especially painful when these people are close family or friends. However, you cannot dwell on these thoughts. While it's natural to hope for understanding from those closest to you, sometimes people lack the capacity to truly empathize or may be grappling with their own challenges.

As challenging as it may be to let go, it's essential for your well-being to surround yourself with those who uplift and empower you. Prioritize relationships that nurture your growth, understanding, and resilience. This doesn't mean cutting ties with loved ones but rather setting boundaries and seeking out individuals who can provide the empathy you need on your journey.

When I was first diagnosed with Huntington's, I thought my world would become smaller. However, I was pleasantly surprised that the opposite was true. I have formed many unexpected friendships with other patients over the years, bonding over shared symptoms and struggles, and my tribe has expanded more than I ever expected.

No matter what challenges you are facing in life, I insist you, too, seek and build your support systems. Maybe start by opening up to a trusted friend or family member. Or you could explore local support groups or online communities. Don't underestimate the strength that comes from knowing that someone else has been on a similar path. Here you find guidance, a listening ear, or a simple, comforting presence.

4. Celebrating Milestones

Another way I keep my spirits lifted through difficult times is by celebrating every milestone, no matter how small it may seem. I know this may seem juvenile, but my condition has taught me to appreciate everything I can still do. These little celebrations are like rays of light that brighten my day and keep me moving forward.

I remember the first time I was able to clean my home in Cleveland on my own. Back in New York, when my symptoms were completely unmanaged, this would have been impossible. But on that day, I did everything by myself. And yes, completing some chores is an accomplishment. It was a small victory that gave me an immense sense of achievement and fuelled the rest of my day.

So tell me, what is something you accomplished today? Maybe you overcame a fear, finished a task, or simply made it through a tough day. Whatever it was, know it matters. So acknowledge and celebrate it because it is the key to retaining a positive outlook in life.

I know better than most how easy it is to get caught up in setbacks. I have had so many over the years, and on more than one occasion, I have let them pull me down. Yet, even if I went back ten steps, I still managed to take a step forward. And I have learned to appreciate that little bit of progress because I made it happen.

So, whether it's a small step or a giant leap, remember that every milestone is a cause for celebration. It's a wonderful reminder that you are an empowered individual, capable and strong, able to find joy even in the most daunting circumstances.

5. Self-Care as a Priority

Self-care is an interesting concept that I feel is somewhat lost to our generation. Growing up, we were taught that working hard and never quitting was the only way to succeed. You weren't supposed to take a day off.

You weren't supposed to stop because it was a sign of weakness. After completing one life goal, you were supposed to move on to the next and then the next. But this relentless pursuit of success came at a cost: our emotional and mental well-being.

In a society that values constant productivity, the idea of self-care may appear counterintuitive, but it is, in fact, the only way to heal our mental and emotional health. Embracing self-care doesn't mean you are quitting or giving up. It is more like resetting and rejuvenating so we can perform at our best in the long run.

Self-care is the act of honoring your body, mind, and spirit, nurturing them with love and attention. In my experience, it has meant finding a balance between rest and activity, listening to my body's cues, and respecting its limitations. Ways I practice self-care include establishing daily routines that prioritize sleep, nutrition, and low-impact exercise. I've also found solace in mindfulness practices, which help me stay grounded and focused on the present.

I encourage you to incorporate some form of self-care into your life. It is not selfish. It is self-preservation. Start by setting some time aside to focus on yourself. It could be ten minutes or an hour, just as long as it is uninterrupted time. Put your phone on silent and do whatever makes you feel good. You may want to meditate, stretch, re-visit a hobby, indulge in some skincare, or just lie back with your eyes closed. It is completely up to you. There is no one-size-fits-all approach to self-care. All that is important is that you discover what works best for you and make it a priority.

Then, when times get tough, these moments of self-care will be like an oasis, distracting you from the hardships around and giving you the strength to get through those dark days.

Final Thoughts

As I pen down these final thoughts, a profound sense of gratitude washes over me. The opportunity to share my story, my experiences, and my perspective with you has been an incredible privilege.

I want you to know, without a doubt, that you are not alone in your struggles. Life has a way of testing us in unique and often unexpected ways. Still, the beauty lies in our collective resilience. Just as I've shared my journey, there are countless others who are navigating their own paths, facing their own battles, and finding their own victories. You are part of a vast community of individuals who understand what it means to persevere, adapt, and thrive despite life's hurdles.

As you embrace your own journey, be courageous. Know that every challenge you face is an opportunity for growth and self-discovery. Embrace change, celebrate your milestones, find your tribe, and prioritize self-care as a means of fortifying your resilience.

I want to express my heartfelt thanks for reading my story, and for allowing me to be a part of your life, even if only briefly. I leave you with this message of hope – the human spirit is capable of extraordinary feats. No matter the circumstances, there is always a path forward, and there are always reasons to hope and believe in the possibilities that lie ahead.

About the Author

Tanita Allen is a writer and motivational speaker with Huntington's Disease from Cleveland, Ohio, where she currently receives treatment for her condition.

An advocate for self-empowerment, Tanita's own journey in confronting her diagnosis amidst the challenges of being a Black woman is an inspiration.

Not only managing her condition, but also caring for her mother, who shares the same struggle, Tanita embodies unwavering determination and compassion.

She aspires to become a motivational speaker who uplifts and guides others through their adversities. Using her own experiences, she demonstrates how faith, resilience, gratitude, and self-determination can create a fulfilling life despite the most daunting circumstances.

Bibliography

Andrew, S. E., Goldberg, Y. P., Kremer, B., Telenius, H., Theilmann, J., Adam, S., et al. (1993, Aug). The relationship between trinucleotide (CAG) repeat length and clinical features of Huntington's disease. Retrieved from National Library of Medicine: https://pubmed.ncbi.nlm.nih.gov/8401589/

Cheon, S.-M., Chan, L., Kam Yin Chan, D., & Woo Kim, J. (2012, October). Genetics of Parkinson's Disease - A Clinical Perspective. Retrieved from National Library of Medicine: https://www.ncbi.nlm.nih.gov/pmc/articles/PMC4027661/

Gusella, J. F., Wexler, N. S., Conneally, P. M., Naylor , S. L., Anderson, M. A., Tanzi, R. E., et al. (1983, Nov). A polymorphic DNA marker genetically linked to Huntington's disease. Retrieved from National Library of Medicine: https://pubmed.ncbi.nlm.nih.gov/6316146/

HDF. (n.d.). Huntington's Disease in Venezuela. Retrieved from Hereditary Disease Foundation: https://www.hdfoundation.org/venezuela

Clifford, F. (July, 1996 3). Utility to Pay $333 Million to Settle Suit. Retrieved from Los Angeles Times: https://www.latimes.com/archives/la-xpm-1996-07-03-mn-20787-story.html

Cohen, P. (2020, June 24). Roundup Maker to Pay $10 Billion to Settle Cancer Suits. Retrieved from The New York Times: https://www.nytimes.com/2020/06/24/business/roundup-settlement-lawsuits.html

Rabin, R. C. (2017, August 22). $417 Million Awarded in Suit Tying Johnson's Baby Powder to Cancer. Retrieved from The New York Times: https://www.nytimes.com/2017/08/22/health/417-million-awarded-in-suit-tying-johnsons-baby-powder-to-cancer.html

White, M. J. (2003, May). Understanding the Asbestos Crisis. Retrieved from Yale Law School: https://law.yale.edu/sites/default/files/documents/pdf/white.pdf